GREAT TRAIN WRECKS

of
EASTERN PENNSYLVANIA

Charles J. Adams III   **David J. Seibold**

Exeter House Books
Reading, Pennsylvania
1992

GREAT TRAIN WRECKS
OF EASTERN PENNSYLVANIA

FIRST EDITION
©1992 Charles J. Adams III and David J. Seibold
ISBN 1-880683-01-6

For information, write:
EXETER HOUSE BOOKS
P.O. Box 8134,
Reading, PA 19603

PRINTED IN THE UNITED STATES OF AMERICA

GREAT TRAIN WRECKS
of
EASTERN PENNSYLVANIA
≈≈≈
TABLE OF CONTENTS

THE CAMP HILL WRECK
July 17, 1856

BOTH THE HUMAN DRAMA AND THE MECHANICAL POWER OF TRAIN WRECKS CAPTURED THE IMAGINATION OF THE PUBLIC, WHICH WAS "TREATED" TO GRAPHIC DEPICTIONS OF TRAIN WRECKS IN THE NINETEENTH CENTURY. (TOP) RESCUERS COME TO THE AID OF UNINJURED PASSENGERS IN HELPING LESS FORTUNATE VICTIMS; (BOTTOM) A REPRESENTATION OF THE MOMENT OF IMPACT OF THE TWO TRAINS NEAR MODERN-DAY AMBLER.

FOREWORD
by the Rev. Philip K. Smith

Railroads have a deep and abiding fascination. Brave surveyors mapped mountains and wilderness, blazing trails that eventually reverberated with sounds of graders and tracklayers, bridge builders, drillers, powder men, rock men, dynamite blasts, mules and horses. After ballast was laid and rails were spiked down, new sounds came: Chuffing of engines; melodious passenger chime whistles; shrill freight whistles that loosened the fillings of those who stood too close, but whistles that signaled rear-end crews in cabooses, sometimes 150 cars behind the tender.

Railroads serve shippers. Railway Post Office cars delivered mail with clockwork precision to cities along main lines and to towns and villages on meandering branch lines. Freight trains carried everything from bulk commodities like coal, wheat, lumber, and petroleum to silk from the Orient, livestock, and machinery. Freight depots took deliveries of china and tractors, clothing and furniture, even prefabricated houses ordered from Sears catalogues. Railroads linked the country with the city, mountains with the plains, the Atlantic with the Pacific.

And yet, a railroad was local. Children waved to their hero, the brave engineer. A train ride was a special occasion. My grandparents and my parents took great pleasure in riding from Hamburg to Reading Terminal, Philadelphia, showing me the wonders of breakfast at the Horn & Hardart. At Christmastime we enjoyed the wonderful electric Christmas Card and majestic organ music in John Wanamakers. We visited Gimbels, returning to store our purchases in lockers in the terminal. During summers, we went to the Franklin Institute, always winding up in Railroad Hall, marveling at the P & R Rocket, People's Railway No. 3, and the 1:8 scale live steam G-1sa Pacific No. 111 made by craftsmen in the Reading shops.

1

Oh yes, we also rode the cab of massive Baldwin No. 60,000. All of them are still there. Before we left, we'd walk past Reading Terminal, turn left on 11th Street, and visit William Becker Hardware and Nicholas Smith Trains, two old-fashioned Lionel dealers in small, tightly-packed stores now lost to urban renewal.

When did you ride the train? Where did you go? What did you see?

I remember the Hamburg station. We arrived about 7:30 a.m. We went under the high umbrella roof to the front door. The waiting room had smooth, wide wooden benches. I wouldn't sit. I was too excited.

A bell rang. Passengers gathered their belongings. Out we went, in time to see the headlight come around the curve, then glide away from us, following the wide, superelevated curve along the Schuylkill (SKOO-kill or SKOO-kull) River, above Miller Concrete with green trucks and yellow lettering.

The engineer waved. The conductor ALWAYS cleaned the handrails with a rag and put down a yellow metal stepstool. With a hiss of releasing air brakes and a low rumble, the train would slowly start to move. Soon I'd see my home in Berne. We'd soar 64 feet above the Schuylkill on Peacock's Lock Bridge at Tuckerton, it's stone arches casting gray shadows on the river in early morning, with the train moving on the bridge in silent gray rectangles.

At Reading Terminal, we'd sway over endless switches, reminding us of our rocking gait through the Seventh Street Cut in Reading. We never did hit those stone walls, but it was close.

Leaving Reading Terminal after dark, we'd look down on thousands of car lights, bright and gleaming coming toward us, soft and red going away. The train rode smoothly on track well-kept by hundreds of men.

Nothing gives you a sense of time, a sense of place, like a train.

Perhaps you didn't ride. Perhaps your family

worked in the vast Reading Shops, building and repairing locomotives and cars, where Niles 225-ton capacity overhead cranes picked up whole locomotives. Perhaps your place is the shops and circular roundhouse in St. Clair, the switchback near Williams Valley Junction, or the Gordon Planes.

A railroad is personal. Trains touch people. In this book you'll meet ordinary people in extraordinary circumstances: Mary Johnson Ambler, heroine of the Camp Hill Wreck; P & R Vice-President Gustavus A. Nicolls and air brake inventor George Westinghouse, Jr., both of whom survived train wrecks; Exeter Station Agent William Lutz, his wife and daughter, Sallie, who rescued passengers from the horrible Exeter Wreck for two exhausting days; conductors, engineers, firemen; even members of the Duke University football team.

The first story in this book ("How Ambler Became Ambler") includes a broadside about the wreck, the first in a long and colorful series of railroad folk songs. These country ballads were inspired by train wrecks, natural disasters, events that received extensive media coverage, and excitement, lure and loneliness of life on the rails. Such songs usually begin on a festive note. Subsequent verses offer hints of impending disaster, though people are blissfully unaware.

When disaster strikes, it is described in graphic detail, concluding with words of comfort or a moral. These songs are the subject of an excellent article: "Railroads & American Music," by Anthony W. Reevy, in the *National Railway Bulletin*, Volume 56, No. 5, 1991, pp. 4-19, available from the National Railway Historical Society, P.O. Box 58153, Philadelphia, Pa. 19102 for $2.00 each (shipping included).

Railroads bring people together, to remember, to share, to know that they take part in an important and vital organization. Keeping trains rolling is not simply a job or even a duty. It is a way of life based on honor, commitment and cooperation.

In the words of St. Paul, "For God did not give us a spirit of cowardice, but rather a spirit of power and of love and of self-discipline" (2 Timothy 1:7).

Pastor Philip K. Smith
Christ Lutheran Church
Stouchsburg, Pa.

ALLENTOWN BRIDGE COLLAPSES, TRAIN IS WRECKED
July 21, 1858

TRAIN WRECKS WERE BIG NEWS FOR THE MAGAZINES OF THE NINETEENTH CENTURY. THIS ENGRAVING OF A WRECK ON THE LEHIGH VALLEY RAILROAD BECAME FODDER FOR THE PEN OF AN ARTIST IN FRANK LESLIE'S ILLUSTRATED NEWSPAPER.

A TERRIBLE WRECK!

BEFORE PHOTOGRAPHY, A PEN-AND-INK DRAWING WAS WORTH A THOUSAND WORDS. IN THIS ENGRAVING, AN ACCIDENT ON THE PENNSYLVANIA CENTRAL RAILROAD IN THE 1850s IS GRAPHICALLY DEPICTED.

GREAT TRAIN WRECK TALES
OF
EASTERN PENNSYLVANIA

PREFACE

It was a romantic time. A time when the glow of a lantern shined as a sharp reflection upon a gleaming steel rail; when the haunting whistle of an approaching locomotive echoed through the countryside; and when conductors barked their orders over the muffled roar of eager passengers and the heavy panting of a behemoth locomotive.

It was a time, as well, when death and destruction followed in the wakes of trains which slid or leaped from their tracks due to natural or man-made aberrations.

This time--this "golden age of steam," as it has been called--has been etched in America's images and legends as a time somehow more simple and more unhurried. It is recalled in misty memories and musty pages and is glorified on celluloid.

But on paper, film, and in the mind, the filth, the cinders, the noise, the back-breaking and soul-starving labor and living conditions have been shrouded by the smoke of time and reality.

This book does not serve to dispel the romantic images of the glory days of railroading. The typical rail journey was without serious incident, and in many ways, the images are true to form.

But there was a darker side to the golden age of steam. Human drama played out in stories which, as you read them, stretch the bounds of human imagination. Leave the railroad history books for the historians. Leave the technical tomes to the technicians.

This is a book for the rest of us--we who enjoy an old-fashioned, captivating tale of drama, tragedy and terror.

Within these pages are accounts of hundreds of

harrowing accidents which have struck fear into the hearts and minds of rail travelers for more than a century and a half.

Despite these events, and the thousands of lives which have been lost as the result of railroad accidents, railroad travel is presently and always has been relatively safe.

The Association of American Railroads recently boasted that railroad shipping is approximately one-sixth safer than over-the-road truck shipping. The association based that claim on comparative accident reports per miles traveled.

Indeed, few if any major rail accidents were recorded from about 1830 to 1853. This is due to the facts that there were few passenger lines in service that early on, and trains traveled at a mere twelve to 15 miles per hour on very short runs.

For historical purposes, there is some dispute over when and where the first American train wreck took place.

It is known that several passengers were injured and one died later of his injuries in a November, 1833, accident on the Camden and Amboy Railroad in New Jersey.

In that accident, caused by a broken axle, former president John Quincy Adams escaped injury, and industrialist Cornelius Vanderbilt sustained severe bruises.

It is generally regarded that 1853 was the turning point for safety (or, in many cases, lack of safety) in American railroads.

Two decades into its growth, the railroad industry was surging ahead with many promises and promotions, but lagging sadly in maintenance within its primitive and aging infrastructure. Technology was introducing faster and heavier equipment, but it was rolling over frail trackage, bridges and ballast.

Lack of employee training and a generally cavalier

attitude toward its customers led railroad companies down the dangerous road toward tragedy. The inevitable was to happen, and the initial euphoria over "safe" rail travel turned into stark fear on the part of many who read headline after headline about railroad disasters.

Newspapers and magazines covered railroad business and accidents with the zeal the media has more recently taken out on airlines. From the board room intrigue to the drama on the rails, America's railroads became convenient kindling to fuel the fires of journalists.

It is interesting to note, and it will be fairly easy to do so as you read through the pages which follow, how the nature of railroad accidents changed over the decades.

At the start, accidents were largely the result of ill-conceived mechanical devices or poorly-designed rail beds.

Then, greed and mismanagement became culprits as railroads became giant corporations which exercised great influence on government, the media and the psychology of a growing nation.

As automobiles and trucks took to their roadways, rail accidents involving these modes of transportation became more prevalent.

And, as the railroads faced decline, neglect and disrepair crept in again as chief factors.

Lurking behind each of these have always been the elements of human error and human frailty. Be it fatigue, alcohol or drugs, these very basic weaknesses have often been cited in train wrecks throughout the decades.

We shall touch on these causes, and their effects, in the forthcoming stories, but it is a mood, not a method or motive, we shall seek.

As I write this, the bleat of a Conrail freight sounds and bounces off the face of Neversink Mountain as the train winds around a horseshoe curve at Klapperthal, along the Schuylkill River south of Reading.

It is a haunting sound, almost an audio anachronism smothered by the rumble of trucks along a nearby highway.

Still, the sound of the train whistle never fails to bring to my mind a wide-eyed wonderment. No matter how sophisticated we as individuals or as a society may become, that sound is stirring.

As the freight snakes in the shadow of the mountain, it enters the same stretch of former Pennsylvania & Reading Railroad track a special train from Harrisburg roared along on May 12, 1899.

Doubtlessly, it sounded its whistle at Klapperthal. Moments later, it was to crash violently into the Cannonball Express, which was pausing at the old Exeter station.

More than two dozen men and women were sent to their graves that night.

While researching that story for a local history book, I was prompted to look further into the train wrecks of the region. The study became an obsession.

After compiling eleven books which recounted legends, ghost stories and tales of shipwrecks and adventure on the sea, a book on train wrecks seemed somewhat of a logical extension.

There is a very real difference between a shipwreck and a train wreck. Except for the trained and adventurous scuba diver or undersea explorer, the site of a shipwreck remains remote and largely inaccessible.

Conversely, one may easily find and visit the places where trains derailed or collided, and the images of the horror which played out at that scene may be brought back to mind by those who scrape away the trappings of today and transport their imaginations back to the time of the incident.

Death and destruction aside, the train wreck is a magnificent event. Tons and tons of iron, steel and wood are splintered and twisted in an overpowering instant. Massive machines are crushed like soda cans. Human lives are changed forever, or ended.

Within the following pages are such stories of accident and agony, crime and punishment, carelessness and carnage, heroism and horror. This book does not intend to be a history book, but is instead a collection of stories designed to fire the imagination and capture some of that dark side of the "romance of the rails."

America has always had a fascination for its railroads. Progress has relegated much of the lore of the rails to melodrama, song and legend.

The stories in this book are neither fiction nor legend. They are true accounts adapted from contemporary reporters, witnesses and documents, and need no enhancement.

It is no stretch of the truth to liken the topics of previous writings on ghosts and shipwrecks to disaster on the rails.

Indeed, as I stand alongside the tracks at the old Exeter (now Lorane) station, the ghosts of those unfortunate souls seem to wander the dusty platform and the rusty rail of the siding. The wretching screech of steel-on-steel seems to rise from the ballast, and the dim flash of a red lantern seems to bounce off the trees.

Those specters, real or imagined, eternally inhabit this and other wreck scenes the world over. They remain not as threatening spirits, lost in a netherworld and doomed to wander in their ethereal existence forever.

They dwell in those places more as pitiful wraiths, victims of sometimes unfathomable anguish and pain at the hands of fate.

Just as the power and mystery of the sea has spawned some of the world's finest and best-known literature and drama, so, too have railroads been the settings for some of the most endearing and enduring tales of all time.

Mark Twain, Charles Dickens, F. Scott Fitzgerald and Rudyard Kipling are among those who have used railroads and those who ride on them and work for them as key players in their works. Dickens, whose "The Signal-Man" is a classic tale of horror along the rails, was himself the victim of a wreck.

The immortal author was shaken up in a June 9, 1865, accident in Staplehurst, Great Britain. While his injuries were comparatively minor (ten people died in the mishap), it is said he never fully recovered from them, and they contributed to his death exactly five years, to the day, later.

And, of course, trains have been glamorized in popular music from their inception. The railroad folk song has survived every trend and taste, and the men and machines of the rails have been glamorized by composers and artists in rhythm and blues, folk, rock and other forms of popular music.

What you are about to read is a chronological account of some of the more noteworthy railroad accidents and disasters which occurred in eastern Pennsylvania from the end of the Civil War to the 1990s.

For this book's purposes, "eastern Pennsylvania" is defined roughly as between the Susquehanna and Delaware Rivers.

That, of course, covers much railroad territory, and includes the thousands of rail miles which fanned out across the Commonwealth from the gentle plains of the lower Delaware Valley into the rugged Appalachians.

It also includes one of the most exciting regions in railroading history. It is a region where the paths of the mightiest rail lines crossed in a dizzying web of steel.

Cities such as Scranton, Reading, Bethlehem and Philadelphia were in many ways dependent on the railroads for their growth during the nineteenth century.

Throughout the commonwealth are towns which came into existence solely because of the railroads. In the western part of the state there are two towns named Colver and Revloc. It is not difficult to realize that Revloc is Colver spelled backwards. It is very interesting to know that the two towns marked the terminals of the Cambria & Indiana Railroad. The towns' names were derived from the first three letters of Mr. Coleman and the last three letters of a Mr. Weaver.

Near Harrisburg, the vast Enola yards were so named because when the yards were established by the Pennsy, the site was so remote that its sole telegrapher called it Elona, which is "Alone," in reverse.

Delano, on the Mahanoy Mountain in Schuylkill County, was Railroad Town before it was named for the Delano brothers, who owned the nearby coal mines. Owned by the Lehigh Valley Railroad, Delano was the site of large yards, locomotive shops and more than a thousand residents who owed their very livelihoods (and, in some regards, their lives) to the LVRR.

Indeed, the name of the once-mighty Reading Railroad still survives, if only on Monopoly game boards. While the decidedly unromantic and generic lines such as Amtrak and Conrail took the place of failed companies, the liveries and legends of the great railroads of the east have lived on through the tireless efforts of generations of railfans who have perpetuated them.

Rail traffic ran at a frantic pace as the region worked overtime to supply coal, steel, and other vital goods for the Industrial Revolution.

Therefore, as this activity played out in dozens of cities and towns and dozens of main lines and spurs, accidents were bound to happen.

Some incidents will be recounted in the briefest of terms; some will be included not so much for their enormity but for their importance to their time and place; others will be presented in great detail because of their sheer magnitude.

As you read the stories, perhaps the faint whistle of a distant train will sound in your head. Perhaps you will visit the site of one of the tragedies and stand in awe at the drama which once played out there.

Too often, these disasters, and the people who were a part of them, have been forgotten through the generations. It's time to pass them on again.

I hope you enjoy the stories.

Charles J. Adams III

13

8 DEAD, 38 HURT IN CRASH OF TRAINS ON CROSSOVER AT BETHLEHEM STATION

EXPRESS HIT BROADSIDE

Engine of Jersey Central Flyer Plows Into the Lehigh Limited.

DEAD ALL IN ONE CO.....

Steel Car Topples in ...... as Smash Comes W..... Shrieking Whistle....

ENGINEER BLAME....

But Lehigh Offici..... of Central Pass..... Running Ahea.....

ES A GREAT WRECK'S SHADOWS

NG NORRISTOWN PLUNGED IN GRIEF OVER HER SIXTEEN DEAD.

AL FIVE FUNERALS TO OCCUR TO-DAY

FIREMEN WILL FOLLOW CHIEF SLING-
LUFF'S BODY TO THE GRAVE.

H INQUESTS BY TWO CORONERS

RIGID INVESTIGATION INTO THE COL-
LISION AT EXETER

Norristown, May 15.—The pall of death
which has fallen over this town as a result of the disastrous wreck on the Reading Railway at Exeter on Friday has not
yet lifted, and it will be months before
the scars have disappeared from the memories of the families so suddenly stricken.
On the streets the sole topic of conversation is the disaster, and the survivors of
the wreck

Dreadful Railroad Accident!

8 Persons Killed and Many Injured—
Residents of Reading among
the Victims.

One of those dreadful railroad accidents which are liable to ...

NINETEENTH-CENTURY READERS WERE KEPT INFORMED OF EVERY DETAIL OF A TRAIN WRECK IN LENGTHY, GRAPHIC STORIES WHICH FOLLOWED STARK HEADLINES IN NEWSPAPERS ACROSS EASTERN PENNSYLVANIA.

GREAT TRAIN WRECKS OF EASTERN PENNSYLVANIA

PART ONE

THE NINETEENTH CENTURY

THE ACCIDENT REPORT

Accident Report—Local No. 2520

ACC... No. ...
TERRITORY No. ...

THE PHILADELPHIA & READING RAILROAD COMPANY.

ACCIDENT to Coal Train, No. _____ at 7.15 o'clock A. M.
Oct 20 1891 Reported Nov 11 1891

Nature of Accident, Conductor injured & Engines & car damaged

Place where Accident happened, Engle Mill switches, near Pt Carbon
(Give name of nearest Station.)

Engine No. 419 Engineer, J. Floar

Conductor, O. H. Post Fireman,

Brakeman, Frank Sands Brakeman,

Cause of Accident, See remarks

Description of Damage to Engine, See remarks

Estimated cost of Repairs of do. $ 115.00

Description of Damage to Cars, See remarks

Estimated cost of Repairs of do. $ 50.00
(Give separate estimate for each Car.)

Crew of Engine 171

Human Life Lost, Engr. James Wenzel
(Give name in full, age, and residence.)
Firman Harry White

Cond'r Chas. Miller

Personal Injury Sustained, Bkman H. J. Snyder
(Give name in full.)
" Jno. Grigor
" Wm Sier

Cattle Killed, value $ _____ owned by _____

Names and Residence of Witnesses,
(Give only in cases of accident to persons or private property.)

REMARKS: Engine 171 was sent to Middleport for light cars by Yard Master Saybold, when engine 171 was up, Yard Master Bull sent engine 419 up for light cars. Yard Master Saybold failed notify Yard master Bull that he had sent engine 171 up.

When collision occurred Charles Miller conductor age 28 residence Pt Carbon jumped from the train and sprained his back. Member of R.R.

Yard Master I. H. Saybold or suspended for one month

_____
Asst Genl Supt

HOW AMBLER BECAME AMBLER

July 17, 1856
Wissahickon, Montgomery County

While the time period generally covered in this volume will be the Civil War era to 1990, there were train wrecks reported sporadically in the eastern portion of Pennsylvania well before the War Between the States.

An early accident was reported on the Penn Central Railroad on February 7, 1856, but no injuries were reported.

The railroad bridge at Easton was the site of a fatal accident on August 28, 1856, when two persons were killed there; and on July 22, 1858, the engineer and fireman of a down train were killed when a bridge over the Little Lehigh collapsed and sent ten cars of a freight train tumbling.

The wreck we shall use as the baseline for this book was, for all practical purposes, likewise a landmark in railroad history. The date was July 17, 1856, and the place was a quiet Philadelphia suburb then called Wissahickon. The story is fraught with every horror known to early railroading, and an act of heroism which changed that quiet suburb forever.

It was about five o'clock on a morning which would prove to be a sultry summer day in the Delaware Valley.

At the Master Street Depot in Philadelphia, some 1,500 pupils, teachers and parents from the St. Michael's Roman Catholic Church poured onto twelve cars on two excursion trains. It was to be a fun day at a picnic grove in Fort Washington, north of the sweltering city.

15

The passengers were loaded with their picnic baskets and the boarding process was long and tedious. Alfred F. Hoppel, conductor of the first train, tried to hurry things along, but the first train, behind the locomotive Shackamaxon pulled out of the station late.

Hoppel was confident, however, that he could make up for lost time along the North Penn route. He was aware that a down train was on its way from Gwynned on the single track, but he knew its schedule. Ironically, it was his regular run.

He mentally calculated the timing of the southbound and northbound trains, and felt the trains could utilize a long siding at Edge Hill, where one could safely cross the other's path.

At the throttle of the Shackamaxon was Henry Harris, barely 21 years of age. Apparently at Hoppel's behest, he proceeded toward Fort Washington at a fair speed, to make up for lost time at the depot.

William Lee, engineer of the Aramingo, which was pulling the down train from Gwynedd, knew of the northbound excursions, but he and William Vanstavoren, the first year conductor of the regular run, also felt they could negotiate the passing safely.

To that end, Lee urged his locomotive along the long grade and into the blind curve at Camp Hill at a delicate speed. As the train slowed to an estimated ten miles an hour, Lee sounded his whistle incessantly. Due to the primitive communications of the day, he had no real way of knowing the exact disposition of the northbound train.

The crews of both trains believed they were in the clear. Between the Camp Hill and Fort Washington stations, early that July morning, they found that their estimations were horribly wrong.

The excursion train, with conductor Hoppel and engineer Harris truly believing that the down train was safely in the Edge Hill siding, rolled along at about 35 miles per hour. The down train inched its way south.

By the time each engineer caught sight of the other oncoming train, it was too late.

The Aramingo and the Shackamaxon locomotives plowed into one another in a sudden, horrible crash. The Aramingo's boiler exploded. The explosion could be heard five miles away. The first, then the second, and then the third cars of the excursion train tumbled forward and virtually disintegrated.

While most of those in the rear cars of the excursion and all aboard the down train were only shaken or slightly injured in the collision, the unfortunate passengers in the first cars of the excursion suffered quick but horrible deaths.

The messenger of death had come to call so early that morning in Wissahickon, Pa. That area would never, in the most literal sense, be the same again.

When the crushed and/or incinerated corpses were sorted out, 59 lay dead. Nearly twice that number sustained serious injury.

William Vanstavoren, the conductor of the down train, watched in agony as the bodies were removed from the smoldering wreckage. William Swaim was an eyewitness to the crash. "A number of the dead were lying in a heap so dreadfully burned that you could not tell whether they were men or women," he said.

Most were young boys and girls who arose that morning with visions of a happy summer picnic tossing about in their minds. Those same boys and girls now were but seared, scarred and disfigured bodies.

While reports of the wreck were rife with horror stories and grisly details of the corpses and the damage, one astonishing tale was told by a Pennsylvania Inquirer reporter:

> *A little, feeble infant was found in the ruins*
> *of one of the cars, piteously crying for its mother.*
> *No mother appeared to answer the summons. She*
> *was doubtlessly crushed to death.*
> *Quick as thought, Mrs. G., one of the boarders*

THE CAMP HILL WRECK
July 17, 1856

TALES OF HEROISM AND COMPASSION SPRANG FROM THE TRAGEDY NEAR THE CAMP HILL STATION, NORTH OF PHILADELPHIA, WHEN TWO TRAINS COLLIDED, KILLING 59 AND INJURING TWICE THAT NUMBER. IN THE TOP ILLUSTRATION, A WOMAN IS SEEN NURSING AN INFANT WHOSE MOTHER WAS MISSING IN THE WRECK. BELOW, BODIES OF VICTIMS ARE PLACED ON MAKESHIFT SLABS IN A BLACKSMITH'S SHOP.

at Bitting's Hotel, seized the little sufferer and
placed it to her own breast, and there, under
the burning rays of the sun, this woman, robbing,
perhaps, her own infant of its nourishment,
was sustaining this orphan, while all around
was noise and confusion, and groans, and
suffering, and death.

Vanstavoren felt somehow responsible for it all.

After seeing all he could stand, he hired a carriage to rush him home. Within hours, he himself was dead. He could not live with the visions of death he had seen. He chose to swallow a fatal dose of arsenic.

In later testimony, Engineer Lee said he had asked Vanstavoren if he had received any orders. It was revealed that the conductor of the down train was instructed to delay his train 15 minutes to give way to the excursion. Lee had noticed Vanstavoren hurrying passengers aboard at Fort Washington, where milk cans were also placed on the train. At that time, Vanstavoren told the engineer he had no orders, and against his better wishes, Lee pulled out of Fort Washington, with a sneaking suspicion that something was awry.

Lee said he sounded his whistle all the way down the tracks, and traveled at a very slow speed. As he brought the Aramingo into the curve, he saw the smoke of the Shackamaxon in the distance, and knew that his worst fears could be realized. As the locomotives bore down upon each other, crewmen leaped, and tragedy ensued.

No one person, nor one element of the short journey of the church excursion train that morning could be blamed for the crash.

In fact, a coroner's jury later placed most of the blame on conductor Hoppel. Observers knew, however, that the primitive state of communications and signalling between trains and stations at the time, was the real grim reaper that fateful morning.

In somewhat tragic irony, the coroner's jury fully

A CONDUCTOR IS INDICTED

Montgomery ~~~~~

Manslaughter

In the Court of Oyer and Terminer for the County of Montgomery, at November Term, in the year of our Lord One Thousand Eight Hundred and Fifty-Six.

The Grand Inquest of the Commonwealth of Pennsylvania inquiring for the County of Montgomery, upon their oaths and affirmations, respectively, do present, That Alfred F. Hoppel, late of the County aforesaid, yeoman, on the seventeenth day of July, in the year of our Lord one thousand eight hundred and fifty-six, with force and arms, at the County aforesaid, in the and within the jurisdiction of this Court, in and upon one *Henry Carr* being unlawfully and feloniously, did make an assault, and the peace of God and of the said Commonwealth, then and there riding, and being upon a certain locomotive steam engine and train of cars thereto said Alfred F. Hoppel, then and there riding, and being upon a certain locomotive steam engine and train of cars, the said lo-attached, and having the guidance, direction and control of the said locomotive steam engine and train of cars, then and comotive steam engine and train of cars, in and upon the said *Henry Carr*

there unlawfully and feloniously, did drive and force and him the said *Henry Carr* did driving and forcing as aforesaid, did with the locomotive steam engine and train of cars aforesaid, then and there by such driving and there, with the wheels thereof, him, throw to the ground; by means whereof the said locomotive steam engine and train of cars aforesaid, did, then and the said *Henry Carr*, neck, breast, back, stomach and arms of him, the said *Henry Carr* so thrown to and upon the ground as aforesaid, divers mortal fractures, bruises and wounds, of there strike upon the head, neck, breast, back, stomach and arms as aforesaid, divers mortal fractures, bruises and wounds, of thereby then and there giving to him the said *Henry Carr* then and

in and upon his head, neck, breast, back, stomach and arms aforesaid, do which said mortal fractures, bruises and wounds, the said *Henry Carr*, in manner and form there instantly died : And so the Inquest aforesaid, inquiring as aforesaid, upon their oaths and affirmations aforesaid, do say that the said Alfred F. Hoppel, him, the said *Henry Carr* aforesaid, feloniously and unlawfully did kill and slay, contrary to the form of the Act of the General Assembly in such case made and provided, and against the peace and dignity of the Commonwealth of Pennsylvania.

ON NOVEMBER 22, 1856, ALFRED HOPPEL, CONDUCTOR OF A SPECIAL TRAIN WHICH COLLIDED WITH ANOTHER PASSENGER TRAIN NEAR THE CAMP HILL STATION, NORTH OF PHILADELPHIA, WAS CHARGED WITH MANSLAUGHTER BY A MONTGOMERY COUNTY CORONER'S JURY. ABOVE IS A PORTION OF THE ORIGINAL DOCUMENT.

exempted Vanstavoren from any real blame in the head-on collision. In an inquisition dated July 25, 1856, Montgomery County coroner Daniel Jacobs wrote, "We deem it due to the memory of William Vanstavoren, the conductor of the down train, since deceased, to state that he was running his train at the time of the collision in accordance with the regulations of the road."

Vanstavoren's own conscience, however, had already indicted, convicted and punished him.

The coroner's findings further stated, "We find that William L. Lee, the engineer of the down train, is free from all blame, and did all in his power to avert the catastrophe after the first warning of the impending danger."

The 12-man inquest panel was direct with its indictment of Hoppel. "We find that the immediate cause of the collision," Jacobs wrote, "was the gross carelessness of Alfred F. Hoppel, the conductor of the excursion train, in running his train contrary to his intructions after it had got so far behind time as to render it his duty to keep the track clear for the regular down train."

Later that year, Alfred Hoppel was arrested and charged with voluntary manslaughter.

A witness said he saw Hoppel read a slip of paper which contained the orders the down train was to follow. That witness claimed to have seen Hoppel put the note back in his pocket and gasp, "My God, why didn't Bill wait his fifteen minutes?"

On February 16, 1857, Hoppel pleaded not guilty to the charge, and later was acquitted, as it was determined there were no clear-cut regulations on the railroad which controlled the passage of excursion trains.

The collision garnered national and worldwide headlines, and was by far the worst train accident in the United States up to that time.

The wreck also resulted in a cultural response to railroad accidents that was new to America.

Broadsides with poetic and lyrical commentaries on

political and social issues were fairly common in Europe for hundreds of years. Those which found their way into the hands of Americans in the Colonial, Revolutionary War and post-war eras were nearly all of a political nature.

Following the Camp Hill crash, however, the wreck of a railroad train for the first time inspired broadsides. Some historians feel they were the precursors of train wreck folk songs and ballads, which later lofted people like Casey Jones and fast locomotives such as The Old 97 into legendary status.

Within days of the wreck, while the stench of its deadly impact was still in the air, the grisly verses were set in type, printed, and distributed to a curious public.

The J.H. Johnson Cheap Card and Job Printing Office, in Philadelphia, published a handbill with the cumbersome title, "Verses on the Death of Miss Annie Lilly, One of the Victims of the Accident on the North Pennsylvania Railroad":

Kind reader, view this happy throng
Of merry children, bright and gay
With teachers, parents, tender friends
Start to enjoy a holiday.

Their merry faces seem to say
The city has no power to-day.
But with our swings, our hoops, our play,
We'll spend a glorious holiday.
And mid the laugh, the jest, the song,
The whistle sounds, the train moves on.

But oh! what means this sudden jar?
This wild confusion in the cars.
These shrieks that now assail the ear,
And fill the stoutest hearts with fear!
What flames are those, that now arise!
Those dying prayers, I'll ne'er forget,
"Have mercy, God!" the trains have met!

RAILROAD DISASTER BROADSIDES

THE KILLED BY THE ACCIDENT

ON THE

NORTH PENNSYLVANIA RAIL ROAD,

July 17th, 1856.

Rev. DANIEL SHERIDAN,
HUGH CAMPBELL,
ANNA LILLY,
JAMES McINTYRE,
BARNEY GREEN,
SARAH McGUIGAN,
JOHN DUGAN,
JOHN RIVERS,
JAMES HICKEY,
JOHN SHAW,
WILLIAM HAYWARD,
HENRY HARRIS,
JOHN DUDGON,
JAMES ERNE,
FRANCIS McCART,
KATE McGEE,
JAMES CONGDON,
HENRY HARLEY,
EDWARD HALL,
ELLEN CLARK,
HUGH TRACEY,

DANIEL MARLOW,
LEWIS BIXEL.

HENRY CORE,
SALLY McGEE,
JOHN McGRAW,
JAMES CONLIN,
MARY O'DANIELS,
THOMAS BARNEY,
JOHN DEVLIN,
EDWARD GILLEN,
PATRICK MICKEY,
JOHN SUGAR,
FRANCIS WALLS,
LEWIS P. FLANEGAN,

(verse text, partially obscured)

VERSES

ON THE DEATH OF

MISS. ANNIE LILLY,

ONE OF THE

VICTIMS OF THE ACCIDENT

ON THE NORTH PENNSYLVANIA RAILROAD.

Kind reader, view this happy throng
Of merry children, bright and gay,
With teachers, parents, tender friends
Start to enjoy a holiday.
Their merry faces seem to say
The city has no power to-day,
But with our swings, our hoops, our play,
We'll spend a glorious holiday.
And mid the laugh, the jest, the song,
The whistle sounds, the train moves on.

But oh! what means this sudden jar!
This wild confusion in the cars,
These shrieks that now assail the ear,
And fill the stoutest hearts with fear!
What flames are those, that now arise!
What horrid screams, and awful cries!
Those dying prayers, I'll ne'er forget,
"Have mercy, God!" the trains have met!

And our Annie was singing
"Do they miss me at home."
When the cars, by a sudden bound
Turned smiles into tears, and life into Death,
And strewed death and destruction around,
Five companions of her youthful heart
The maddning flames did brave,
And nobly did they strive in vain
Our darling's life to save.
'Till forced by flames they must stand by
And see our Annie helpless die.

Must see her burn and cannot save
Even her bones to fill a peaceful grave;
Cut off in youth, so young, so soon,
With ne'er a coffin, grave, nor tomb.
But parents bow to Him above,
At whose right hand reclines your love—
No earthly pains distress her now,
No shade of care is on her brow.
Yes, happy were her earthly days,
She's now the object of the Angel's praise.

J. H. JOHNSON,
SONG PUBLISHER, CARD AND JOB PRINTER,
No. 5 NORTH TENTH ST.,
Three doors above Market, Philadelphia.

CARDS, CIRCULARS, BILL HEADs, &c., &c., NEATLY PRINTED

AFTER THE CAMP HILL WRECK OF JULY, 1856, ENTERPRISING PHILADELPHIA PRINTERS PUBLISHED BROADSIDES WHICH TOLD THE TALE OF THE TRAGEDY IN LYRICAL TERMS.

And our Annie was singing ,
"Do they miss me at home."
When the cars, by a sudden bound
Turned smiles into tears and life into
Death,
And strewed death and destruction around,
Five companions of her youthful heart
The mad'ning flames did brave,
And nobly did they strive in vain
Our darling's life to save.
'Till forced by flames they must stand by
And see our helpless Annie die.

Must see her burn and cannot save
Even her bones to fill a peaceful grave;
Cut off in youth, so young, so soon,
With ne'er a coffin, grave, nor tomb.
But parents bow to Him above,
At whose right hand reclines your love --
No earthly pains distress her now,
No shade of care is on her brow.
Yes, happy were her earthly days,
She's now the object of the angel's praise.

Even more graphic were the 13 verses of another broadside which was published after the wreck. The names of four dozen of the victims were grouped beneath the headline, "The Killed by the Accident of the North Pennsylvania Rail Road."

Although the senses of the public were tormented by the deaths of the innocent young passengers of the St. Michael's Church picnic train, there was one redeeming legacy of that July morning.

In rail history terms, the wreck has been recorded mostly as the Camp Hill Wreck, because of its proximity to the Camp Hill Station of the North Penn Railroad, which 13 years after the wreck was to become the

24

Bethlehem branch of the Reading Railroad.

In regional terms, the site of the accident may be better identified as Wissahickon, and Ambler.

We say *"and* Ambler," because that name was not given to the tree-shaded suburb until after the wreck, and as the somewhat indirect result of the wreck.

Within minutes after the impact of the two locomotives, a woman rushed to the ghastly scene with bandages, medical supplies, inestimable compassion and inexhaustible energy.

From that early morning, well into the night, she worked tirelessly to comfort the injured. She opened her home as a makeshift hospital.

She was a Quaker, a widowed mother of nine, the founder of a Sunday School in her home, and the operator of a fulling mill her late husband had established. It was felt she was somewhat of a "powwow" practitioner, a sort of faith healer.

As the summer heat sweltered, the woman worked feverishly to save who could be saved and comfort those who would die. Neighbors carried injured passengers to her place on litters fashioned out of window shutters. She administered her aid for hours on end without stopping for food or drink.

Officials of the railroad were so impressed by and grateful for her aid that they offered to pay her for her time and trouble. She declined.

Neighbors were likewise impressed, and when it came time to change the name of the Wissahickon Station because another stop in Philadelphia already had that name, the angel of mercy's name was submitted as a nominee.

She was up against tough competition. Wissahickon could have become Reiff, after Joseph Reiff, who donated much of the land upon which the railroad right-of-way was built.

It could have become Thomas, or a variation, after Isaac Thomas, who was a miller, postmaster and shop owner there.

It could have been named after William Harmer, an early settler.

But it was eventually named after the heroine of the Camp Hill Wreck. On July 20, 1869, a new station was dedicated, and in 1888, a new borough was established, both bearing the name of Ambler, after Mary Johnson Ambler.

Mrs. Ambler never knew of her distinct honor. She died in 1868, and was buried at the Gwynedd Friends Meeting House cemetery.

HER HEROICS WERE REMEMBERED

MARY AMBLER WORKED TIRELESSLY TO AID THE INJURED IN THE CAMP HILL WRECK OF 1856, AND AFTER HER DEATH, THE VILLAGE OF WISSAHICKON WAS RENAMED IN HER HONOR.

WAR ON THE RAILS
July 15, 1864
Shohola, Wayne County

The Civil War reared its ugly head on the rails near Shohola, Pike County, in the summer of 1864.

In what is regarded as the worst train wreck of the war years, 65 men lost their lives in a head-on collision between two trains which met on a sharp curve early in the morning of July 15.

Most of the victims were Confederate prisoners who were being transferred from a ship which had brought them from the battlefields to Jersey City, N.J. They were being transported to a prison camp in Elmira, N.Y.

The 18-car train was due to leave the port city along the Erie Railroad at 4:30 a.m., but a handful of prisoners could not be accounted for as the train was about to depart.

After a thorough search by Union MPs, the stowaways were discovered still in the ship.

The delay may have been a primary cause of the ensuing accident.

At Lackawaxen, Pa., a telegraph operator assured a downbound, 50 car coal train that it could proceed safely toward Port Jervis, N.Y. The coal train was switched from a branch onto the main line, unaware that the delay in Jersey City had skewed the schedule of the army train.

Both trains rolled along the single track, assured that even with the primitive signalling and communications, they were in the clear.

Aboard the army extra were some 800 prisoners of war, 125 guards and the train crew. When the dust settled, the debris was sifted and the dead were counted, 51 prisoners, 10 Union guards and four crew members became war casualties, far from the fields of battle.

***

October 14, 1865
Near Lancaster

As was wont to happen in the early days of railroading, a broken axle led to disaster along the Pennsylvania Railroad line between Lancaster and Harrisburg.

The trip was unremarkable for the day express that crisp, autumn day. The train was on schedule, and there were no problems until the axle snapped, the train careened, and four cars tumbled from the tracks.

Among the eight persons who perished in the crash was Ann D. Barr, wife of James P. Barr, the surveyor-general of Pennsylvania.

***

March 9, 1867
Temple, Berks County

The quiet station at Temple, five miles north of Reading, was the site of a grisly, freak accident which cost the lives of two young women.

The two had intended to board the train at Temple and head into the city. They made their way to the platform only to find out that the southbound train had already left.

They decided to walk into Reading along the rail line. Not far from the station, at the crossing of the Eastern Railroad, they heard the sound of an oncoming train.

The girls attempted to flee the rails, but one of them got her right foot caught in the cowtrap at the crossing. As her friend attempted to release her, the train bore down on them and they scrambled underneath it as it lumbered along.

One died almost immediately, horribly mutilated in the accident. The other passed away later of internal injuries.

***

August 14, 1869
Dauphin, Dauphin County

In the 19th century, two modes of transportation and shipping drew headlines when accidents happened. For investigative, and perhaps insurance purposes, a maritime accident was considered an "act of God." Railroad accidents were described as the fault of man.

That assessment could well be tossed out the window in the next account.

Even today, and despite all precautions taken, falling rocks and landslides in railroad cuts and along rail lines perched precariously on the edge of a mountain pose a real danger.

Just north of Harrisburg, the railroad tracks and highways are sandwiched between the Blue Mountain and the Susquehanna River. Braces, walls and barriers have been built to protect vehicles on both rights-of-way. The prospect of rocks tumbling from the edge of the hillside is still a threatening one.

In the latter half of the 19th century, the thin sliver of flat land known as Dauphin Narrows was creased by the Millerstown Pike, the canal, and the rails of the Susquehanna and Schuylkill Railroad.

The Buffalo Express and Erie Mail Train had departed Baltimore the night before and passed through Harrisburg at 3:15 in the morning, pulling some passenger and mail cars and several other cars filled with peaches and assorted cargo.

While hemmed in with dangerous cliffs on one side and a 20-foot drop to the highway on the other, the Dauphin Narrows provided a fairly straight stretch railroaders called an "air-line."

At such areas, any lost time could easily be made up at maximum speed.

While a slight fog hung over the tracks that morning, engineer Charles Wesley Stewart saw a clear track ahead as he and fireman Lemuel Crisman put the big Northern Central engine through its paces.

At once, the train's cowcatcher grinded into what was described as a rock of at least a half-ton. The boulder had rolled from the mountainside and onto the tracks, apparently dislodged during a rain storm the previous evening.

For about 100 feet, the engine plowed and pummeled the rock. Ties cracked beneath and the rails twisted until the momentum of the locomotive and the tormented track caused the engine to tumble over a steep embankment, over a stone wall and onto the Millerstown Pike.

"One baggage and three express cars, and the tender, like the lash to a whip, flew past the locomotive," a contemporary news account described, and two of the cars fell into the canal.

But for what was later described as a "miraculous escape," many passengers may have died or suffered that morning.

As the express cars and tender piled onto and around the fallen locomotive, one passenger car, completely filled, got no farther than the stone wall.

It dangled perilously, supported solely by rail which had been wrenched from the ties. About 20 feet below was the roadbed, and probably certain death for many of those in the car.

The conductor maintained strict order, and instructed the panicked passengers to gingerly find their way to safety.

A news dispatch the next day described the scene: "How the men who were in the cars that went over the embankment escaped it is impossible to tell. The passengers on he train only appreciated their providential escape after leaving the cars. Had the whole train gone over the embankment, the loss of life would have been fearful."

As it was, only engineer Stewart and fireman Crisman were killed in the wreck. Crisman, who was reportedly due for a promotion to engineer within days, was crushed under the locomotive.

A coroner's inquest immediately after the accident concluded that the Schuylkill and Susquehanna Railroad deserved the blame for the wreck, "for not keeping a watchman constantly on duty at the point...deemed dangerous in the estimation of the jury."

***

February 1, 1872
Mud Run, Carbon County

The name "Mud Run" has taken its place in railroading lore in eastern Pennsylvania.

While the tiny flag station north of Mauch Chunk (now Jim Thorpe) was a speck on the railroad map, it looms large in legend as the site of one of the most disastrous wrecks in regional history.

That wreck will be addressed in coming pages. This story pales in comparison.

Still, it represents the horror of how inferior material, when combined with natural conditions, can bring death and destruction.

The Lehigh Valley R.R. train was northbound in the early morning hours on a frigid February day. The weather weakened a rail that snapped beneath the weight of the locomotive.

The engine and baggage car passed safely over the fractured rail, but the steel buckled as the two passenger cars reached it.

The first car spun off the track, down a 40-foot embankment and into the Lehigh River. The second left the tracks, rolled over several times, and came to rest at the foot of the embankment.

One of the most feared consequences of cold-weather travel then took place in the wrecked cars. The stoves which had provided warmth and comfort to the passengers set the wooden debris on fire, and within moments, eight passengers were incinerated.

While rescue teams sped to the scene from Mauch Chunk and surrounding towns, the flames and the agony spread.

Many injured passengers were rushed to the Mansion House in Mauch Chunk, where more volunteers offered assistance, but the deadly combination of human and natural conditions had again taken its toll on an eastern Pennsylvania railroad.

* * *

August 16, 1873
Tamaqua, Schuylkill County

The scene was Mitzers' Switch, about three miles north of Tamaqua. The accident was minor, in train wreck terms, but could have been newsworthy but for the kind hand of fate.

A passenger train headed toward Ashland collided with a special train, and although both engines were virtually demolished in the powerful crash, the crewmen sustained only minor injuries.

It is interesting to note, however, that aboard the one-car special train was G.A. (Gus) Nicolls, then vice-president of the Philadelphia and Reading Railroad Company.

He survived with nary a scratch, and continued to serve as one of the most colorful executives in the railroad's history.

WRECKERS ON THE RAILS
September 23, 1878
Auburn, Schuylkill County

The fierce and bloody strike of 1877 was behind, but considerable bitterness remained among employees caught in the iron-fisted tactics used by the Philadelphia and Reading Railway to bring a swift and certain end to the dissention in its ranks.

The company had exacted a costly price as it smashed the clandestine Molly Maguires organization in the coal towns and literally stopped strikers throughout the system dead in their tracks.

The Mollies were a terroristic offshoot of the Ancient Order of Hibernians, and their hostility toward the railroad and coal mine owners grew out of a deep-seated animosity born in their native Ireland. Their hope for better living and working conditions in America had not been realized, and their frustrations were unleashed in a trail of murder and violence from the 1850s to the 1870s.

Finally, Franklin Gowen, president of the P & R, hired Pinkerton security agents to infiltrate the ranks of the Molly Maguires and bring an end to the acts of violence against mining and railroad authorities. Pinkerton raised a veritable private militia which would meet the Mollies on their own terms.

Gowen, himself an attorney, aided in the

spectacular trials which brought the ringleaders of the Molly Maguires to justice. One by one, the leaders of the group were sent to the gallows. The last to hang was the alleged Molly mastermind, "Black Jack" Kehoe, in 1878.

Then, it was on to new challenges for the Reading and Gowen. But, to many folks in the patch towns and flag stations across the Pennsylvania coal regions, memories of the Molly Maguires would not fade quickly.

Through the summer of 1878, reports of deliberate attempts to wreck trains on the Reading lines were numerous.

Little damage was done, but one incident came close to causing great suffering.

While there was no evidence that connected James Hurley to the Mollies or any of the anguish of previous years, it was noted prominently in the press that the 40-year old was an "Irishman."

Hurley had been a flagman at Auburn, but in July, 1878, he was accused of random acts of vandalism against railroad property. He was ultimately fired by his section foreman, and made immediate threats of revenge.

Early in the evening of September 23, 1878, Hurley was noticed wandering near the switch at Auburn. The witness who saw him later told investigators that when he challenged Hurley, he shouted back, "Don't stop me or I'll kill you!"

Within minutes, an eight-car passenger train rolled toward the Auburn Station. What should have been a safe passage turned into terror as the engine and several cars careened off the track. The switch had been closed.

Miraculously, while there was considerable damage to the train, there were no serious injuries to any of the 300 passengers.

Railroad officials, well-schooled in responding to acts of suspected sabotage, were quick to probe the incident.

A special train with railroad executives, a squad of special police, and two private investigators was dispatched to Auburn. They captured James Hurley and remanded him to Pottsville for an immediate hearing, and eventual conviction.

THE DRAMATIC CAPTURE
OF A TRAIN WRECKER
May 16, 1883
Ephrata, Lancaster County

It was a scene right out of a wild west movie.

But it was no farther west than eastern Lancaster County.

It all started harmlessly enough. Just another fourteen-year old boy hopped just another freight train.

He was Jacob Gangaway, and the train he boarded was a freight which left Ephrata on the Reading and Columbia Railroad the afternoon of May 16.

The train was between Millway and Rothsville when the front brakeman discovered the stowaway and chased him from his free ride.

The lad, described later as a somewhat dimwitted, tousled rascal who spoke with a thick Pennsylvania Dutch accent and was large for his age, was infuriated, and vowed to have revenge.

In a confession to police, Gangaway acknowledged that he left the train, ran ahead and was inspired to commit what turned out to be a fatal act of vandalism.

He noticed a large plank next to the tracks at the end of a deep, curving cut in the roadway, about a mile and a half north of Ephrata. The plank was later measured at about 18 inches wide, four inches thick and 12 feet long. At the time, he said, he felt he could "have some fun," place the board across the tracks in front of the oncoming freight, and gain his vengeance.

He anchored the plank firmly with large rocks, and positioned himself on a bridge where he could watch the result of his malicious handiwork.

Engineer Alexander McConnell was bringing his train of twenty cars into the cut at about 25 miles per hour. He was running at full throttle to gain enough speed for an upcoming grade. The position of the obstruction was such that it was not easily seen from the cab until the last second.

McConnell watched incredulously as the plank suddenly appeared, and he called "down brakes," in an effort to avoid what would be an almost certain catastrophe.

As the locomotive screeched along the rails, momentum carried it into the roadblock. The board was so well placed that it caused the engine to leap four feet from the tracks, teeter some 20 yards, until it leaned against an embankment and rolled on its side into soft ground.

McConnell was thrown over the top of the cab, and his fireman and conductor managed to leap to safety. But George M. Hain, the master mechanic of the Reading and Columbia, was not so fortunate.

Although he was thrown from the train upon impact, the engine rolled over onto him. In the indelicate phraseology of 19th century journalism, a news dispatch reported that Hain "was slowly roasted alive, being able to speak to those who could not rescue him while he suffered his last agonies."

Hain was pinned under the firebox a full 45 minutes. His legs were being burned away, but he remained semi-conscious. In his dying gasps, he moaned what he had hoped would be rescue instructions to his fellow railroaders, until death put him out of his misery.

A scheduled passenger train arrived at the site an hour later, and was flagged to a stop while emergency crews assessed the damage to the freight.

One of the passengers, Charles Geiger, of Reading,

later described the wreck scene. "There was nothing left of the engine but the boiler," he reported. "Some of the wrecked cars were thrown up on the bank 20 feet and piled on top of each other. All were tossed about as if they were mere playthings."

Geiger, and the other passengers were hustled past the grisly scene, and had to walk to Ephrata to make further connections.

As word spread to the cities and towns of Berks and Lancaster counties about the deliberate wreck, many people made no secret that they favored an immediate lynching when and if the perpertrators were found. The railroad quickly vowed to use all its investigative powers to find the villains and bring them to justice.

After his heinous deed, Gangaway reportedly was noticed by a nearby farmer who had heard the rumble of the accident from the cut. The farmer saw that the boy was running from the vicinity of the tracks, and asked him if he had any knowledge of a derailment. He rudely dismissed the question and ran from the farmer.

Later, in a full confession to authorities, Gangaway said he was disappointed because from his perch on the overpass at the time of the crash, he could not see the results of his sabotage because of the smoke which billowed from the locomotive.

Gangaway was later implicated in the act of "wrecking," and charged with manslaughter in the death of Hain, but not until a most spectacular capture.

In the 1870s, the deeply-wooded ridge which straddles Lancaster and Chester Counties was a fairly remote and forbidding place. While it was somewhat of a misnomer, owing to its relative size, that ridge was (and is) called the Welsh Mountain.

Legends still abound in that area of the desperadoes and alleged horse thieves known as the Buzzard brothers who once held their ground on the Welsh Mountain.

Described variously as bona fide "outlaws," feeble-minded "hillbillies" and unfortunate outcasts, the Buzzards nonetheless gained a notoriety unmatched by any other gang at the time, and quite possibly, since that time.

Acting on a tip, Marshal Joseph Heisler and officer Boone of the Philadelphia and Reading Coal and Iron Police, ventured into the forested fortress of the Buzzard brothers, where they had learned that Jacob Gangaway, who had been fingered as the chief suspect in the Ephrata wreck, may have been holed up.

Based on local lore, they could not have expected an easy time of it as they went for their prey.

They were responding to a clue provided by a logger at the base of the Welsh Mountain. He told them that a boy who had been working for him fit the description provided by the farmer who saw the suspect fleeing the wreck scene. In addition, that boy had left the logging camp with his meager possessions just prior to the time of the wreck.

The detectives posed as drovers in search of a young boy who might be looking for ready employment tending stock.

They managed to track down what they believed to be Gangaway's family cabin. They were met by the boy's mother and stepfather, who seemed to sense they were not really cattlemen.

Feeling they were on the wrong track, they next headed toward a sawmill, where they again received no help in their investigation.

Sure enough, as the detectives closed in on the place Gangaway was supposedly in hiding, they learned that he was being given protection by the Buzzards, or some of their compatriots.

Boone and Heisler approached the suspected hideout cautiously, and were promptly pelted with a volley of stones and threats from a large crowd of people. Two men jumped the detectives, knocking them to the ground. They rebounded, and stood their ground.

As they managed to withstand the first assault, the detectives were surprised when two rather large and rather vicious dogs were set upon them. Stones do not give chase and have teeth. Dogs do.

The officers later testified they were forced to resort to their pistols for self-protection against the dogs and the small mob.

Determined to "get their man," Boone and Heisler made another stab at breaking through the outlaws' line of defense, but were again turned back.

Finally, they noticed a young man who fit Gangaway's description being spirited deeper into the woods by three or four other men.

They plotted their attack, flanked the suspects, and moved in, pistols drawn and cocked.

They finally captured Gangaway in a marsh, and although three of the ne'er-do-wells made an attempt to free him, the officers' revolvers staved off that final rush.

It was at the marsh, near Red Run, where Gangaway, with tears streaming down his face, told the detectives that he indeed was put off the train that day, and was on the bridge when the wreck took place.

Gangaway was taken to Reading, where he offered a full confession, was locked up overnight and then transported for a formal hearing in Lancaster.

By the beginning of June, Ganaway's escapade had gained national attention. The New York Times printed a daring editorial which recounted the wreck, the capture, and what it called "a failure of justice."

The unsigned commentary could only have made the reader concerned about whatever kind of "justice" the author was seeking:

> *Impartial people, intent only on the upholding of the laws, hoped that this uncommonly atrocious crime would be punished so severely that its repetition would never be attempted. Did the people of the region where this innocent man* (**Hain**) *was murdered rise en*

41

masse,storm the jail, and hang the murderer? Or
was he speedily tried and "railroaded" to the
penitentiary? No: he was admitted to bail in
a small amount and is now at liberty to wreck
more trains and take the lives of other innocent
and estimable men. This is what people outside
of Pennsylvania call a failure of justice.

A rather daring stance, indeed. And, it did not go unnoticed.

Two days after the call for a kangaroo court and necktie party, one L.K.Witmer, who had recently left his native Lancaster County for a job in New York City, responded to the Times' editorial.

Witmer lambasted the credibility of the Times, and went on to point out that despite the sensationalistic accounts of the wreck and the capture of Gangaway, "...the boy was arrested without any difficulty, there being neither mountains nor outlaws worthy of those names anywhere within that region."

Witmer continued, "The people 'failed to rise up en masse, storm the jail, and hang the murderer' simply because of the fact of his feeble-mindedness, which was conclusively shown by the testimony of reputable physicians at the preliminary hearing."

It can be conceded to Witmer that the Welsh Mountain has been misrepresented, but how the tales of the Buzzard family had eluded him is anyone's guess.

Obviously provincially-proud and literate, Witmer concluded his letter to the editor, "I only desire to shield the home of Thaddeus Stevens, James Buchanan, Robert Fulton and John F. Reynolds from calumny."

The trial of Jacob Gangaway began in Lancaster on October 25, 1883. The suspect, who was described as detached and apparently unaware of the seriousness of the manslaughter charge against him, pleaded not guilty at his attorney's prompting.

There were suspicions from the very start that the

target of Gangaway's wrath was not the freight train, but the later passenger train which followed. That was never proven to be the case.

What was proven was the prosecution's case against Jacob Gangaway.

The defense tried everything to impress the jury. Gangaway, the attorney said, was the product of a pathetic family. He had two uncles in the Lancaster County insane asylum, and while the boy was not insane, he was too "weak-minded" to stand trial. Also, according to his lawyer, Gangaway suffered epileptic fits.

The lad's age, 14, was also entered as a defense. His lawyer pleaded the court to dismiss the charges because he was a juvenile.

The most compelling defense, however, came from Gangaway himself. He was called to the stand, and speaking in the Pennsylvania German dialect through a translator, claimed that while he had been at the scene of the wreck, he did not place the plank on the tracks. He saw the crash, but ran from the scene in fear.

In fact, he said, his confession was forced. He contended that officer Boone threatened him at the time of his capture, and told him to admit his guilt.

The broad-ranging defense made little impression on the jury. After only about 90 minutes of deliberating, the twelve men returned with the verdict.

Jacob Gangaway: Guilty of involuntary manslaughter in the death of Master Mechanic George M. Hain.

FIRE AND RAIN
October 4, 1877
Kimberton, Chester County

The year 1877 was one of turmoil in the railroad business.

A bitter strike of the Brotherhood of Locomotive Engineers spread death and destruction throughout the region, and by summer, random acts of vandalism and sabotage had made their way into railroad stations and trains, causing fear and suspicion among passengers and railroad employees alike.

On October 4, newspapers in eastern Pennsylvania reported a flurry of fatal accidents up and down the rail lines. One, near Melrose, Susquehanna County, was blamed on a wanton act of sabotage by strikers.

An engineer was scalded to death and the fireman crushed under the tender when a fast freight on the Delaware and Hudson line was derailed by a closed switch.

But another very real threat to safety on the rails swept the region that day.

Near Frenchtown, N.J., three people were drowned when an express train bound for Philadelphia was washed off the tracks and into a river.

At about the same time, somewhere north of Coatesville, the engineer of a Wilmington and Northern passenger train bound for Wilmington was killed when his engine overturned on a section of track washed out by a heavy downpour.

But the most significant train wreck to follow in the wake of the torrential rains took place near Kimberton, on the Pickering Valley Branch of the Philadelphia and Reading Railway.

The accident made headlines not only for its magnitude in terms of human drama and trauma, but also for the personalities who were involved.

The weather that night was miserable when the three-car train pulled out of Phoenixville at about 6 o'clock.

Dark clouds cast a dismal pall over town and country, and the incessant rainfall had caused many streams to overflow their banks.

About 130 passengers were aboard the train, which was headed for the end of the line in the village of Byers. Most of them were homeward bound after a day of festivities at a reunion of the Pennypacker family in Schwenksville.

The descendents of Heinrich Pennypacker, one of the first settlers in that part of the Delaware Valley in the early 18th century, had gathered for meetings and luncheons. Folks from all over the nation found their way there that day, and as it turned out, those with the least distance to travel back home that night were to suffer excruciating horror.

Engineer Frank Kenney inched his locomotive through the storm, well aware that such rainfalls could well result in flooding and track washouts.

Without warning, the earth under the wheels of the engine gave way, and the big machine tumbled into a chasm 30 feet deep.

Kenney and his fireman, George Griffith, were killed instantly. The first, and then the second passenger cars followed the engine into the muddy hole. The end of the second car remained on the track elevation, and the

45

conductor managed to scramble from the wreckage to a nearby farm house.

From there, he borrowed a horse and went into Phoenixville to summon help.

As the rains continued to pelt the scene, survivors worked to remove the injured to the baggage car, which had remained on the tracks. Dozens of passengers were hurt, and seven were killed.

By 8:30 p.m., a relief train found its way through the storm to the scene and doctors stepped in to treat those in need.

The list of casualties was crowded with Pennypackers, as their joyous reunion that day had turned into a night of terror.

An investigation of the accident determined that it was caused by the extraordinary weather conditions that night.

The embankment over which the train had traveled was considered safe under normal conditions. Water coursed under the track through a French drain during ordinary storms. That night, however, the rain was so intense that the resulting washout had carried about 60 feet of track away.

The railroad was chastised for installing bars across the windows of the passenger cars, and for placing the milk and baggage car in the rear of the train. But generally, the coroner's jury agreed that the wreck was "unavoidable," considering the circumstances.

"...ROASTED TO DEATH WHERE HE STOOD!"
April 5, 1878
Slatington, Lehigh County

On April 5, 1878, the residents of Slatington must have thought Lucifer himself had come to town.

The crack of dawn brought with it a fury that stands as one of the most bizarre and fearsome accidents in the history of eastern Pennsylvania.

Lehigh Valley Railroad engine 154, pulling 40 oil tankers and four boxcars, was southbound from Mauch Chunk as it approached the Slatington Depot at about 20 miles per hour.

Neither engineer John Watmore nor fireman Irwin Mosser saw any indication that trouble was waiting for them.

But, a freight train which had left Mauch Chunk earlier in the morning was forced to pull up at Slatington when its engineer noticed a hot journal. He intended to remain there until the bearing cooled down. That, most certainly, was never to happen. The freight was stopped at the depot, its crew either unaware of the oncoming oil train or falsely confident that precautions had been taken to warn it before it reached Slatington.

While nothing was ever conclusively decided, the crew of the later train claimed there was no lantern on the stationary freight's caboose which would warn them to stop. Chances are, even if a warning signal would have been displayed, there would have been no time to avoid the inevitable.

Engine 154 lumbered directly into the tail end of the standing freight, and all Hell, literally, broke loose.

The oil train's locomotive slipped from the tracks, exploded, and within minutes the flames ignited the tank cars.

Thick, black smoke spiraled into the early morning sky, and the rumble of explosions could be felt throughout Slatington. Flames and the glow of fire could be seen for many miles. Earwitnesses say the explosion sounded like a very, very loud clap of thunder.

It wasn't long until the flames licked the walls of a nearby foundry and machine shop, and spread toward the railroad depot and nearby rowhomes.

A large crowd had gathered to fight the fire, and although the foundry was consumed, the depot and houses were saved.

Many buildings in Slatington suffered broken windows as the powerful concussion rocked the valley. An oily mist fed by the estimated 60,000 gallons which blew up spread over at least a full square mile. Large chunks of the engine and tankers were tossed as far away as 300 yards.

In one of the most bizarre incidents, a piece of the firebox of Engine 154 was propelled about 100 yards, through the roof of a home. It landed not far from the bed in which Mr. and Mrs. Jacob Hummel were sleeping. They were obviously shaken by the experience, but escaped uninjured.

While the wind was fanning the flames and spreading the blaze, it was blowing away from the town. It was speculated later that had the wind shifted, all of Slatington may have been in peril.

Quick work by crewmen also prevented any further damage. Those tankers toward the rear of the train were uncoupled and allowed to drift from the fire. And, a local militia company fired bullets into the blazing tank cars so the fuel would escape and lessen the chance for more explosions.

Still, 15 tank cars spilled into the river, and a grimy coating of burning oil floated downstream. A wooded area two miles south of Slatington caught fire as a result.

A contemporary account of the conflagration was vivid in its detail:

> *The shower of fire came so suddenly...that it covered the mass of people before they had a chance to escape. There was a mighty rush for safety, and, choked by blinding smoke and maddened by pain, each man struggled to save himself.*
>
> *When the smoke rolled back, here and there were men flying like madmen with their clothes aflame.*
>
> *William Shoemaker, an old man of 77 years, was not strong enough to get away, and he was roasted to death where he stood.*

The putrid smell of burning flesh mingled with the stench of the oil fire, and one by one, the victims of the freak fire were pulled from the inferno.

Two men were killed almost instantly, four died later of burns and/or smoke inhalation, and more than 50 people were injured. Fire fighters raced to the scene from as far away as Mauch Chunk, and the flames were stilled by evening.

A coroner's jury later exonerated the railroad for any blame in the demise of William Shoemaker, terming it "death by accident."

The incident did change life in Slatington. The growing town, which was physically split into lower and upper sections, was without an organized fire company at the time, and was at the mercy of surrounding fire fighters. That would change in short order.

The April inferno shook the town, compelling it to deal with technologies and dangers of the industrial revolution.

IRON HORSEFLESH
When Rails Crossed Trails

The first time a hissing iron boiler on wheels puffed past a flesh-and-blood horse, a certain trepidation must have swept through the mind of the steed.

As the paths of carriages and trains began to cross in the 19th century, the modes of transportation too often headed on collision courses.

Ironically, rail travel owes much of its development to the horse. Many railroad historians pinpoint February, 1827, as the date rail travel was firmly established in the United States.

It was then, on 14 miles of Baltimore & Ohio rails, when what can be considered our first railroad made its first run--pulled by horses, and on rails made of wood.

Steam engines came along in the next decade, and heady railroad investors predicted their lines would rewrite history and provide a lifeline which would link America's two coastlines.

Of course, stagecoach, canal and boat lines decried the rails as dirty and unsafe, and fought for their shares of shipping and passenger traffic.

But within five years of their inception, railroad companies in the United States totaled about 200. There was no stopping their accession of land, investment money and the public trust.

The first true train "accident" in this country is considered to be an October 8, 1833 "concussion" in New Jersey, which claimed several lives.

Train speeds were slow and cautious at first, and there was almost no nighttime service. As speeds increased and equipment became heavier, construction techniques could not keep pace.

And, as more passengers answered the "all aboard" call of the conductor on more passenger lines, the danger of human tragedy became more real.

In 1852, 42 railroad passengers died in train wrecks. Another 120 railroad employees perished in accidents. In the ensuing decades, those numbers were to spiral higher and higher.

The sheer magnitude of the railroad industry was staggering. By 1890, nearly three-quarter of a million Americans worked for a railroad. In 1920, that figure climbed to 2.1 million. From 1870 to 1930, a period many call the "golden age of railroading," the rail industry dominated the business news, and too often the obituary pages.

One of the most painful transitions in that era was the necessity of the slower and more fragile types of transportation to adapt to the unbridled power of tons of rolling iron and steel.

The passing of a train through town, city or countryside in the early years was cause for much excitement and rubber-necking. And, where rails crossed trails, anything could happen.

The account of a man at the downtown Reading railroad crossing in 1877 provides interesting insight.

"IN THE SHADOW OF DEATH: THE TERRIBLE EXPERIENCE OF MR. ALBERT MILLER IN PITCH DARKNESS BETWEEN TWO TRAINS!" That was the headline over a fascinating Reading Eagle story:

> *The frightful accident at 7th and Penn streets early Sunday morning, while not attending with any serious injuries to Mr. Albert Miller, shows from his account of it, the terrible danger through which he passed. The night was very dark and he*

51

was very careful in looking out for the watchman's signal as he drove near Seventh street.

He says he heard, or thought he heard, the noise of a locomotive approaching the crossing but the watchman's lamp was hanging at the side of the watchbox and he though there was no danger. He was quite near the railroad when the engine of a freight train puffed past. The horse, a four-year old animal belonging to his father, became frightened and rushed forward. The driver took him in hand, tried to turn him around, but failed.

The horse made a jump and struck one of the cars. Mr. Miller says he was sitting in his carriage, a new vehicle worth about $100, and was closely wrapped with robes and blankets when the engine of a coal train came down the road. The engine struck the carriage, broke it into pieces and knocked him out between the tracks just behind the horse.

It was very dark and he says he could not see his hand before his face. He was between two trains and himself, horse and the broken carriage were whirled around and around probably a half dozen times. He could not see a particle and could only hear the crash of the carriage wreck, the groaning of the horse and the clatter of the car wheels over the rails.

Every moment he expected to be ground to tiny pieces under the cruel wheels. Above the noise and confusion he heard the whistle for brakes and knew the cars were stopping. He remained perfectly quiet and was picked up between the two tracks. The horse was led down the street by Officers Moore and Good-fellow and in front of the Eagle office the animal was knocked on the head and killed by one of Mr. Boyer's employes. The horse had been badly hurt.

Thus, the saga of the first accident (and, as it turned out, first fatality) at Reading's 7th and Penn Streets grade crossing was presented to a public which read the story with rapt attention.

Mr. Miller suffered cuts and bruises, and was up and about within a few days. His horse was not as fortunate.

If the meeting of horse and iron horse in the 19th century created dangerous conditions, the prospect of an era which would bring together railroad trains and automobiles would be even more fearful.

Indeed, as the popularity of automobiles and the utility of railroads both grew in the 1920s, the two conveyances too often headed on collision courses.

The Interstate Commerce Commission reported grade crossing fatalities on American highways, and in the peak year of 1928, an average of six persons per day were killed in auto-rail accidents. By 1932, grade crossing deaths began to show a decline.

"More care on the part of motorists, improved warning devices and the elimination of a number of dangerous crossings all had their effect," said J.R. Crossley, vice president of the Automobile Club of New York, in a report on the drop in crossing fatalities in 1932.

In the intervening years, however, thousands of teamsters and then motorists lost their lives at the hands of railroad trains.

THE BOB-TAIL CAR TRAGEDY
October 5, 1883
Philadelphia

A classic example of the fatal clashes at railroad crossings is a mishap which claimed the lives of four persons at Susquehanna and American Streets in Philadelphia.

The intersection is where the Reading Railroad's North Pennsylvania branch and the Union Passenger Railway Co. streetcars crossed the city streets.

It was early autumn, and the streetcar line had gone into its non-peak season schedule, with the car's driver doing double duty as driver and conductor.

Peter Schultz was bringing car No. 408 from Frankford eastbound at about 6:30 in the morning. Fifteen passengers were aboard the horse-drawn streetcar, known popularly as a "bob-tail car."

At Susquehanna and American, the 23-year old Schultz summoned a young boy to tend the horses while he and a woman passenger were inside the car, trying to settle a dispute over her fare.

The boy either couldn't or didn't see the furious motions of a flagman at the railroad tracks, and trotted the bob-tail over several tracks which cross at the intersection.

Suddenly, Laura Bignal, one of the passengers in car 408 looked down the tracks to see the Newtown Express bearing down on them. Her screams alerted the others to the impending calamity.

Frank Bird, engineer of the express, was clanging his bell and the flagman was waving wildly, and both likely expected the streetcar to heed the warnings and hustle across the tracks.

It did not. It was too late.

With a shattering screech and crunch, the train engine plowed into the streetcar. It was no match.

The bob-tail whirled into the air and came down crushed into splinters. The passengers were thrown into an agonizing pile, and their screams attracted neighbors' attention in the early Saturday morning hours.

Help from nearby Episcopal Hospital was summoned, and passers-by helped sort through the split timbers, shattered bulkheads and mangled ironwork of the streetcar to pull the victims out of the wreckage.

Schultz's foot was torn from the ankle. One passenger was decapitated. Not one of them escaped injury. Four never recovered from those injuries.

As would be expected, all parties in the accident were held somehow responsible in the Coroner's Inquest the following week.

The streetcar company was censured for allowing one person to act as driver and conductor; the Philadelphia and Reading Railroad was likewise slapped on the corporate wrist for allowing its trains to run faster than the city speed limit for trains and for employing an incompetent flagman at the crossing.

Further, driver-conductor Schultz and engineer Bird were held criminally responsible for the deaths.

In a subsequent investigation into the accident, it was determined that the railroad had followed the minimal signalling standards as established by the city of Philadelphia.

While safety gates had been required at virtually all other intersections of city streets and the railroad's North Penn division, the affected crossing was not included in the ordinance.

Conversely, a law passed eight years before the accident stipulated that "all passenger railway companies in the city of Philadelphia whose tracks cross any steam railroad at grade, shall, before their cars cross such road, compel their conductors to stop all cars and cross the tracks of such steam railroads in advance of the cars, under penalty of fifty dollars for each and every violation."

The streetcar company tightened its regulations regarding grade crossings and drivers acting as conductors, and the mayor of the city instructed the police chief to enforce the city ordinances more stringently.

But the barn door of safety had been closed after the horse of death had escaped.

RACING THE GRIM REAPER
April 19, 1887
Lancaster

We move four years ahead and sixty miles west for another accident which is indicative of man's temptation to test the speed and power of an oncoming locomotive.

Of course, by 1887, hundreds of people had been killed at grade crossing accidents. Many were victims of their own bravado, derring-do, miscalculation or stupidity.

And, more than a century later, accidents at railroad crossings are still fairly commonplace, as motorists, cyclists and hikers dare to ignore or circumvent signals or are caught unaware at unmarked crossings.

There is no reason John and Catharine Becker, of the Manheim area had to die that April afternoon. The engineer of the Pennsy's limited express said he did all he could to prevent the collision, but to no avail.

The Beckers were returning home from a morning of shopping in Lancaster when they reached the Pennsylvania Railroad crossing along the Petersburg Turnpike at the Lancaster Chemical Company plant.

In their wagon was their daughter-in-law, Emma Becker, and her 15-month old baby.

There were several eyewitnesses to the tragedy, and each confirmed that the express was sounding its whistle as it steamed toward the intersection.

Emma Becker, who survived the crash, said she

heard the train bearing down on the wagon, but did not recall hearing the whistle.

In any case, John Becker whipped his horse in what was to be a fatal race against the big locomotive. The buggy and the express reached the crossing at the same time. The express won.

The wagon was smashed to pieces. Mr. and Mrs. Becker were killed instantly.

Emma Becker, clutching her child, somehow got lodged in the train's cowcatcher. After several feet, she fell onto the roadway.

Miraculously, the 15-month old child hung on as the train carried her another 300 yards before it screeched to a halt.

The baby escaped with not even a bruise. Emma Becker suffered cuts and a broken collar bone. Her in-laws were not as fortunate.

THE MUD RUN DISASTER
October 10, 1888

GRISLY SCENES CAME FROM THE PENS OF SUPERB ARTISTS FOLLOWING MAJOR TRAIN WRECKS OF THE NINETEENTH CENTURY. (TOP, LEFT) BODIES ARE CARTED AWAY FROM THE WRECK SCENE; (TOP, RIGHT) VICTIMS ARE CARRIED TO THE MUD RUN HOTEL; (BOTTOM) BODIES ARE STACKED IN FRONT OF A HORRIFIED CROWD NEXT TO THE WRECKED CARS.

THE MUD RUN DISASTER
October 10, 1888
Mud Run, Carbon County

The last two decades of the nineteenth century were the bloodiest of railroading's "golden age." As roads of steel snaked across the heavily-industrialized eastern Pennsylvania, the propensity for disaster became more threatening.

Railroad accidents were suddenly commonplace, and the toll of freight tonnage and human lives soared.

All factors, from natural to negligence, began to combine in a terrible tally which would keep headline writers as busy as wreck crewmen and coroners.

October 6, 1883; Near Cresco, Monroe County: Engineer John Dunn was killed, along with his fireman, Archibald Lard, as a Delaware, Lackawanna and Western freight train rear-ended a coal train on a steep grade in the Pocono Mountains.

October 6, 1883; Near Barnestown, Montgomery County: A brakeman was killed when five cars of a Pennsylvania Railroad mixed train derailed.

May 5, 1888; Near Locust Gap, Schuylkill County: Seven children and the father of two of them were killed inside their home when a freight train bound from Locust Gap to Williamsport, split into two sections and exploded. A coupler broke between the third and fourth cars of Train No. 67 as it descended a long grade along the Locust Gap Creek.

The first section continued chugging along for

about 100 feet until Engineer Robert Gallagher noticed the separation and called down brakes. As the first section came to a stop, the second section rolled into it.

It was a horrible blunder, considering the third car was fully loaded with gunpowder, glycerine, ignition caps and T.N.T. When the train sections collided, a powerful blast lit up the night.

In a small house next to the tracks, John Quinn and his four children were spending a quiet night together.

Theirs was one in a row of eight tiny houses which were owned by the Philadelphia and Reading Coal and Iron Company, and occupied by miners and their families.

They probably never even heard the commotion on the tracks, which were about one hundred feet up a steep embankment from their creekside "patch."

With no time for escape, the explosion from the train rattled their home, and burning embers showered down upon it in an infernal fury.

The Quinns' cookstove ignited, and hot coals shot like burning bullets in every direction. John Quinn didn't stand a chance. His blackened body was pulled from under the stove, and the bodies of two of his daughters were later pulled from the wreckage. Two other family members sustained serious burn injuries, but survived.

Next door, the horror spread to the home of Mr. and Mrs. Simon Kerwick. They were with their five children when the blaze whipped through their place before spreading to and destroying every home in the row.

Simon Kerwick first saved his sickly wife from the rapidly-approaching flames. He did not have time to save the children. One by one, eight-year old Daniel; five-year old Alice; the adopted Willie and Mary Cavanaugh, ages 14 and 8; and the Kerwick's newborn infant, perished in the holocaust.

Rescue workers from nearby Locust Gap responded quickly and managed to save the residents of the other company homes.

But when the damage was assessed, 13 railroad

cars were reduced to splinters and 17 houses were charred rubble. As far away as in Mt. Carmel, windows were shattered by the force of the explosion. And, it is said that not a single window in Locust Gap survived the concussion from the explosion.

No story, even one as agonizing as the Locust Gap explosion, could have prepared Pennsylvanians--and indeed readers of major news anywhere in America--for the drama and destruction wrought in October, 1888, when what seemed to be a totally avoidable error sparked a chain of events which would rock railroads to the very root of their credibility and shake newspaper readers to the base of their tolerance.

October, 1888: Reports were filtering in from Aspen, Colorado, that the Silver Star Mining Co. had struck a rich vein of silver in the Rockies. Prospectors from across the country began to descend on the town to seek their fortunes.

October, 1888: In the Sierra Madre mountains of Sonora, Mexico, "four bucks, two squaws and two boys" were taken into custody by Federal marshals. They were allegedly the last of Chief Geronimo's renegade Apaches.

October, 1888: Fourteen Sioux Chiefs arrived in Aberdeen, Dakota Territory, on their way to Washington, D.C. Among them were Thunder Hawk, Two Bears, Mad Bear, Big Head, Bear Rib, Grey Eagle, Fire Heart, Walking Eagle, Hairy Chin...and Sitting Bull.

October, 1888: An article in The New York Times told the story of "Pauline McCoy, colored, who was hanged at Union Springs, Alabama, for the murder of Annie Jordan, white."

And, as eastern Pennsylvanians read about a new trade pact between Russia and Corea (sic) and Princeton defeating the University of Pennsylvania, 63-0 in Foot Ball, thousands of people descended upon Hazleton for the annual Union of Father Mathew Catholic temperance Societies' parade and celebration.

From all over the Scranton diocese, the masses

assembled. Especially heavy was the rail traffic to and from Scranton, Wilkes-Barre and the Wyoming Valley. There were some 10,000 members of the societies, a.k.a. The Total Abstinence Union, and nearly every town and village in northeastern Pennsylvania was represented in the Hazleton gala on October 10, 1888.

Several trains, completely filled with participants in the rally and parade, had left Scranton early that morning.

The day's events had passed, and approximately 5,000 celebrants were packing into an eight-section, 87-car Jersey Central Rail Road train which would transport them back to stations along the Lehigh Valley line from Hazleton north.

The first train pulled out of Hazleton at about 5 p.m., and then the second, third and rest followed behind.

It was with the departure of the seventh section of the excursion that calamity would rear its ugly head once again along the Lehigh Valley line.

The eighth section left about ten minutes after the seventh, in accordance with a special policy adopted by the railroad. Normal procedure called for a five-minute span between trains, but the Lehigh Valley mandated a longer headway due to the large number of passengers aboard the Father Mathew excursions. The eighth and last pulled out of Hazleton at the same interval as the rest.

Rollin H. Wilbur, assistant superintendent of the Lehigh Valley Railroad, issued a statement after the disaster, and attempted to explain the situation:

When the seventh section reached Mud Run, the engineer found the signals turned against him, signifying that the ten minutes to intervene between the passing of the train ahead and his train was not up, and he brought his train to a stop, the rear car being about 300 yards from the station. The train was stopped on a curve, but an approaching train in the rear could be seen for a half a mile. Red lights were displayed on

*the rear of the train, and the flagman went back
with his lantern to warn the eighth section.
Despite these signals, and also the one at the
station, the last section, drawn by two powerful
engines, came along and crashed into the train,
telescoping the rear car completely.*

The word, "telescope," was not unfamiliar to railroaders and readers of wrecks at that time. It had come to describe a most violent crash in which the force of a locomotive would drive wooden passenger cars into one another, in a motion not unlike the closing of a telescope.

Until reinforced steel cars came on the line, the "telescope" collision was one of the most deadly on American rail lines.

The cars used on the excursion that day were particularly fragile, even be contemporary standards. In fact, Charles Haines, a passenger aboard the section which crashed into the other, estimated his train was moving at only about ten to twelve miles per hour at the time of the collision.

Anderson Brown, engineer of the train which was struck, testified in a coroner's inquest that he had stopped his section at Mud Run to allow the proper gap between his and the previous section. While waiting, he left the cab and oiled his engine: Standing operating procedure.

As he prepared to step back on the footboard, he caught the headlight of the oncoming section about 300 yards down the track. At that, he jumped into the cab, whistled "up brakes," threw the throttle wide open, and got underway. He said his train advanced about a coach car's length when it was struck.

Albert Calvert was standing on the platform at Mud Run that evening. His statement was particularly incriminating. "I am positive that the engineer (of the last section) could have seen the danger signal had he been on the lookout."

Calvert saw the horrible incident, and testified

that the flagman of the section which had stopped at Mud Run was displaying a red lantern, and another red signal was hoisted at the station itself. Thomas Major, engineer of the second locomotive on the eighth section, said he did not see any signals until he reached the station.

Rumors ran rampant throughout the region that the section which could not come to a complete halt at Mud Run may have been operating without air brakes.

Assistant Superintendent Wilbur was quick to disspel that allegation, but offered a possible reason for the promulgation ofthe rumor. He said the lead engine, a new, heavy-draught locomotive was most certainly equipped with air brakes, while the second engine was not. He said this was standard procedure, and not outside the bounds of safety.

Other allegations were made, leading many folks to believe the railroad was engaging in a cover-up because of its own neglect. One thing for certain, the railroad controlled the telegraph services up and down its lines, and precious little information got through until several hours after the accident. Editorials in several newspapers after the crash lambasted the railroad for its control of the telegraphs, which could have been used to inform the public and victims' families.

Eventually, anguish spread throughout the region as hundreds of people who had heard unconfirmed reports of the accident at Mud Run gathered at the Delaware and Hudson Station in Scranton. Word had reached that city through telegraph connections from Hoboken, N.J., that there were many deaths in a rail disaster at Mud Run.

Until confirmation was made by the Lehigh Valley Railroad, however, the rumor mill was working overtime, with charges and counter-charges.

Some said the engineer of the last section may simply have been dozing at the time of the accident. It was reported he had been on the job for 48 hours without rest.

"This is absurd," said Wilbur. "We have too

65

many engineers on that division to create any necessity for exacting an excess of work from any man."

Wilbur contradicted another rumor. "As to the statement that the man was under the influence of liquor, it is not probable there is any foundation. A man so drunk as to neglect his duties when he got on the engine would almost certainly give some indication of it, and he would not be allowed to climb into the cab of his locomotive. The company is very strict about that."

Harry Cook, of Scranton, was engineer of Engine 452, also known as the "Mill Creek," which crashed into the section in front of it. He jumped from the cab upon impact and sprained his ankle. A Scranton Republican reporter tracked him down at his home after the incident, and Cook vehemently denied he had been drinking or asleep. He also said he saw no signals as he brought his train around the curve and into Mud Run.

Other company officials responded to various other charges which were circulating in the region.

The engineers were familiar with the line, and experienced behind the controls of both freight and passenger trains. No crew member involved had ever been disciplined for any reason, and each man was hand-selected for the excursion runs because of the number of passengers involved.

One top executive of the Lehigh Valley Railroad, which suffered an estimated million dollars in damages, did offer an interesting disclosure. Alexander Mitchell, superintendent of the Wyoming Division, admitted that the induction telegraph system was not in use on the excursion trains. "It would have been a precaution," he told investigators later, "had it been in use."

But it was not in use, and all the hindsight in the world could not have brought back the victims of the Mud Run disaster. After all the inquests and investigations were concluded, the cause of the collision seemed so tragically simple.

Mud Run's little flag station with its cluster of

railroad-employee housing was at the end of a cut through which the tracks were laid, some sixty feet above the Lehigh River.   In the approach to the station is a short culvert and a fairly long curve. At that point, the two sets of tracks narrowed to one. There was a standing order that all trains approach Mud Run slowly.

Veteran Lehigh Valley engineer Luke Kemmerer, who had been the pilot of the second section of the excursion, said that even at thirty miles per hour, he could get his train to stop between the culvert and 150 feet of the station. He said signals at Mud Run were not uncommon, and the red lantern could be seen up to a fifth of a mile away.

While proper signalling had been used between the two trains, nobody aboard the second section was apparently paying any attention. A lookout on the moving train said he saw the danger signal on the standing train up ahead, but said he really had no idea exactly what it meant, and did not report it.

Oh, what misery that gaffe did cause!

Whether or not the eighth section was braking at the time may have been a legal issue, but it meant nothing when the giant locomotive plowed violently into the rear car, No. 216, of the seventh section.

Forty passengers in that last car were supposedly killed in the instant of the impact. Twenty-two more were to die in the moments after the crash.

The cars were shoved and compressed into one another by the overwhelming force of the train engine. They split apart as if they were made of toothpicks. Cars and pieces of cars tumbled down the embankment. Steam spewed from the damaged locomotive, and several people not killed outright were scalded to death as they lay pinned in the wreckage and unable to escape.

It is said the wails and moans of the injured could be heard a mile away, and those who survived the crash rallied to try to save those who were trapped inside the mangled mess.

A contemporary report said that "scattered throughout the wreck were broken musical instruments, smashed up drums and articles of wearing apparel. The wreckage was dyed with blood. The freight house of the little station and the rooms of the humble hostelry that stands on the bank of the creek all bore marks of the terrible work that had been done. Pools of blood, ensanguined bandages and rolls of lint and plaster gave the scene the look of a battlefield hospital."

Rescuers used axes to chop their way through the rubble of what was once a railroad train. In one case, a zealous volunteer chopped off a young woman's leg so she could be pulled from the wreck. She died minutes later.

One of the passengers lived to tell of his experience. "The first I knew of the accident was the sudden and tremendous jarring of the train," said Walter McNichols, who had been sitting in a car at about the middle of the last section.

"Two engines were pulling the train on which I was," he continued. "As soon as the crash occurred, the people who filled the hind train at once rushed for the doors. The jam was fearful. The people went out of the windows pell-mell, and the first I saw was the forward engine of our train jammed right into the hind coach of the forward train. The cars had taken fire from the broken lamps, but the flames were quickly extinguished by the use of buckets. The scenes were fearful. Bodies were wedged in between the seats, and among the broken timbers. One man was held down by the dome of the engine of our train, which had crashed upon him. Another had tried to escape by the windows of the car, but was caught in the crash, and the life squeezed out of him. He was pinned between the timbers."

As the wreckage was cleared and trains could gain access to the scene, the tally of the dead began. A special train filled with Catholic clergymen and physicians, was dispatched from Scranton to the wreck site. Sixty-four bodies were retrieved, and in a grim procession, were taken to mortuaries in nearby towns and cities. Victims were ferried across the Lehigh River to the Leslie's Run station of the Jersey Central tracks, and taken to the village of Tannery.

The grief which gripped northeastern Pennsylvania was incalculable. When word of the disaster reached Hazleton, a dance scheduled for that evening was cancelled. Scarcely a town in the Scranton area did not lose a resident in the crash.

Volunteers manned the railroad stations to which the corpses were delivered. Priests around the Wyoming and Lackawanna Valleys braced to deal with the pain inflicted on their parishioners. The funeral train proceeded along the line, discharging its morbid freight at the appropriate stations. The bodies were partially prepared for burial, and were placed on boards propped on the backs of seats in three coaches. More than 50 bodies were unloaded at Wilkes-Barre, as hundreds of spectators gathered at the station to see whatever it was they wanted to see.

In Scranton, one of those who shared in the miserable task of taking bodies off the trains from Mud Run, identifying them and assigning them to a mortuary was Lawrence Duhigg.

One of the bodies which passed in front of him carried no identification. The face was so gruesomely scalded and disfigured by steam that identification would be virtually impossible. The only shred of information was a badge on the man's coat which linked him with a Scranton branch of the temperance society. Duhigg scribbled "Scranton/Unknown" on a piece of paper and pinned it to the dead man's chest.

Upon one last examination of the body, Duhigg noticed that the man was missing one toe. At almost the same moment, he was informed that his brother, Thomas, was among the missing from the wreck.

Thomas had lost a toe in an accident several years before. The body of the man, whose face was horribly mutilated, was that of his own brother!

The people of Scranton had never, and hopefully will never again, witnessed as solemn a period as what followed in the wake of the Mud Run disaster.

While women and children were among the dead, most victims were breadwinners of the time--miners and laborers who took great pride in their abstinence and were generally pious and upstanding contributors to church and community.

The mayor of Scranton asked all businesses in the city to suspend operations on the morning of October 13, when a massive funeral would take place at St. Peter's Cathedral and proceed to Hyde Park Cemetery.

Black wreaths and bunting draped many doors in the area, and offers of monetary assistance came in from a wide area. Most merchants in Scranton complied with the mayor's request, and agreed to close from 9 a.m. to noon on Saturday, October 13, 1888, so the city could bury its dead. Virtually all mines and mills in the region were also closed that morning.

By nine that morning, every pew in the 8,000-seat cathedral was filled. It was estimated that another 2,000 persons jammed Wyoming Avenue in an overflow. The already hushed throng grew reverently silent as the cathedral bell tolled nine times, marking the beginning of the requiem mass.

Members of the temperance union carried six caskets up the aisle of the sanctuary to the altar, which had been carefully adorned with flowers and lighted candles.

Four priests led the services, with several others positioned around the cathedral to render assistance.

The coffins were then carried out of the church and placed in hearses as Bauer's Band played a dirge.

It was reported that the funeral procession took a full hour to pass by one spot, and the streets from the cathedral to the cemetery were lined with mourners and the curious.

As the hearses from St. Peter's proceeded toward the cemetery, an unexpected encounter took place. The funeral procession of five other victims of the wreck was winding its way from St. Paul's church in another part of Scranton, and also to the Hyde Park graveyard. The two corteges merged into one, continued to the cemetery, where all eleven bodies were prayed over and lowered into their graves.

That Saturday, the 13th, was a day of grief throughout the valley.

In suburban Minooka, eight bodies were buried in that town's cemetery, as another massive crowd jammed the church and funeral procession route.

But perhaps the most moving of all funeral masses held that day was in another Scranton suburb which had been hardest hit by the Mud Run collision.

One writer said, "...the grief there was intense and uncontrollable and such as to unnerve the stoutest heart." Nearly every home was in some way affected by the crash and the deaths it brought.

The Thistle Band of Pittston and the Albion Band provided somber music as priests from several surrounding communities gathered to give their assistance to their colleague at tiny St. Mary's Catholic Church.

That town which had lost 26 of its own that horrible night in the dark mountains at Mud Run could not, not that Saturday morning of mourning, live up to its name...Pleasant Valley.

Today, nothing remains of Mud Run but battered foundations, barely discernible under thick growth along the active Conrail tracks.

To reach what was Mud Run flag station, one must hike several miles down trails within Hickory Run State Park and then along the tracks about two miles in a finger of land which is part of the Lehigh Gorge State Park. It is that remote now, and was even more remote then.

Few in surrounding villages even know there was

ever any such disaster the magnitude of the Mud Run Wreck. Historians in Kidder Township did dedicate a picture and a page of text to the incident in their commemorative anniversary book, but most folks around the tiny town now known as Lehigh Tannery more recall when Brady's Bar was destroyed on January 13, 1974, when a Conrail piggy-back car derailed and crushed the building.

Trains don't stop at Mud Run anymore. The long freights lumber by the site of the old station, their crews probably unaware of the drama, the tragedy, which took place there so long ago.

* * *

October 16, 1888
Tamanend, Schuylkill County

It would seem that following the tragedy at Mud Run, the Lehigh Valley Railroad would have tightened its procedures, and all personnel would have been painfully aware of safety precautions.

Perhaps there was an attempt, but an incident just three days after Scranton and the towns around it laid their dead to rest, yet another train wreck blamed on yet another lapse in signalling claimed eight more lives.

This time, however, the casualties were railroaders themselves.

The accident took place on the Pottsville Division of the Lehigh Valley, when a Pennsylvania Railroad freight train slammed into a Lehigh Valley gravel train which was backing into a siding at Tamanend.

Aboard the gravel train were several recent Hungarian immigrants who were serving as laborers. Six of them were killed on impact, as was the brakeman on that train and his counterpart on the Pennsy freight.

Railroad investigators concluded rather quickly that the wreck was caused by the failure of the gravel train's flagman to run far enough from the rear of his train to give adequate warning to the fast freight.

72

THE PREMONITION
June 23, 1890
Tuckerton, Berks County

Lew Heller spent the better part of that Sunday night visiting his uncle, Lewis Beyel, in Tamaqua. Uncle Lew had been ill for some time, and Heller, an engineer on the Philadelphia and Reading, went from his home in Pottsville to Tamaqua the night before he was to report back to work, running engine 893 from his home town to Philadelphia along the banks of the Schuylkill.

Sitting around his uncle's house, Heller surprised a cousin, Lance Fairer, when he said it may be best for him to stay with Uncle Lew rather than go to work the next day.

As Fairer recalled later, Lew Heller was fearful that his uncle might pass away, and he may never see him again. But Fairer thought it odd when the engineer added, "...and yet, there's no telling. I may die before you!"

Cousin Lance chided Lew for his comment, and assured him that his uncle would certainly survive his illness. Heller went home that night.

A restless night it must have been, however. The following morning, Heller had a difficult time bidding his wife goodbye as he headed for the engine house. He made three false starts out of the house, each time returning for a long embrace. When he finally made it through the front door, he tapped on the living room window and offered his spouse a poignant wave.

Friends reported Lew acted particularly strange that morning as he greeted each of them with a "goodbye" rather than a "good morning," as he usually did as he strode to work.

By nine o'clock that Monday morning, Lew Heller was behind the throttle of the train steaming southbound with a Pullman parlor, a baggage express and three coaches in tow.

Lew's brother, George, was fireman, and Charles Seiders was conductor. The baggage master was George Hamilton.

The trip from Pottsville to Auburn was unremarkable, but connections in Port Clinton held up the 893 several minutes. To make up time, Lew Heller opened the engine up and sped along th relatively straight stretches toward Reading.

He was still about ten minutes behind schedule as he approached Tuckerton. With no warning, the big engine wobbled, rattled, shook and spun from the tracks. The tender separated and was hurtled several yards away, the baggage express and Pullman rolled off the rails and smashed into the engine, and two of the coaches were derailed.

The force of the derailment was such that the engine was whipped around one hundred and eighty degrees and crushed.

In the passenger cars, men and women screamed as broken glass showered down on them and they struggled for their survival.

Miraculously, all did survive. Railroaders later credited the steel-framed Pullman as the saviour. Had this sturdy car not been placed between the locomotive and the wooden coaches, the latter cars may well have telescoped into one another, causing untold deaths.

As it was, those crewmen in the engine and baggage express cars were not as fortunate.

Three mail messengers were slightly injured, and

Hamilton wound up pinned under his desk in the shattered baggage express car. "When I felt the engine going," he said, "I grabbed hold of the strap. It broke and threw me to the floor of the car. Suddenly the huge desk, screwed fast to the partition, was wrecked and knocked off, and it fell upon me just as the trunks were sent all over me in a heap."

George Heller was thrown from the engine and wound up under the forward part of the locomotive. His engineer brother, Lewis, somehow remained in what was left of the cab, and was found still at the throttle.

For many minutes, the Heller brothers moaned as life drained from their broken bodies. By the time Lewis and George Heller were extricated from the wreck, Lewis was dead.

George Heller lived to tell the story of how his brother seemed downcast and dejected during the fatal run from Pottsville to Tuckerton. He felt that Lewis had some kind of premonition that disaster would strike at any time.

In an almost unbelievable quirk of fate, another Heller brother figured in a bizarre incident which followed the Tuckerton crash.

James Heller was a P & R engineer on the Philadelphia-to-Pottsville run that same day.

James and Lew Heller often crossed paths on that run, usually at Royersford.

That morning, however, James brought his train through Royersford, with no sight of his brother's down express.

He later said he had felt odd all morning, as if something terrible might happen. At about ten o'clock, he was swept with the overpowering sensation of gloom. He became nervous and apprehensive.

It was at about ten o'clock that morning when Lewis Heller died in the Tuckerton wreck.

When James Heller's train reached Reading, he was summoned and given the bad news about Lewis and escorted to the hospital to see George. Witnesses say James seemed to take the news of his brother's death calmly, almost as if it was some sort of relief.

The cause of the derailment was traced to a closed switch, and further intrigue followed in the days after the wreck.

It was reported to authorities that the traditional railroaders' pocket watches carried by the Heller brothers were missing. Neither body was mangled, and only a few links remained on Lewis Heller's watch chain. The immediate response by rescuers was that the watches had been stolen.

At that juncture, a series of accusations which a more enlightened populace might find uncomfortable was released to the press.

A front-page news article in the Reading Eagle did not mince words:

> *The thought that the unfortunate men were robbed at the scene of the collision is too horrible to entertain, yet those watches are missing.*
>
> *Of course, no railroad man is suspected. Employees on the road are far too honorable and honest.*
>
> *A number of Italian and Hungarian laborers are employed in that vicinity, and it is said they were the first on the ground after the accident.*
>
> *Nothing has happened in a long while that has caused so much indignation among railroad men.*
>
> *There may have been thieves on the train, and because some foreigners were first at the wreck is no good reason why they should be accused.*

Thus, while the derailment at Tuckerton claimed only one life, the circumstances which surrounded the accident made it noteworthy.

And, the death of Lewis Heller that Monday morning in June could be considered the first in a series of tragedies which would sweep the rails of Berks County in the summer of 1890.

Railroaders had their share of superstitions.

•Any locomotive which had been involved in a wreck became jinxed engine.

•Bad luck would befall anyone who swept out a caboose after sunset.

•Engines with 9 or 13 within their numbers were bad luck.

•The month of September was the unluckiest month for a railroader.

•Train wrecks generally occurred in groups of three.

Those last three beliefs would be factors in the following months in and around Reading.

HORROR ON THE HAIRPIN TURN
August 22, 1890
Reading, Berks County

The Mt. Penn Gravity Railroad was not only an engineering and technical marvel, it was also a leading tourist attraction and source of amusement in the city of Reading.

Promotional literature touted a ride on the "Gravity" to be "as if swaying in a balloon over the green billows below."

"How delightful, how soothing, how refreshing, how grand a beautiful the outlook; how glorious the summer day," the brochures promised those folks who were willing to plunk down two-bits (a dime less for kids) for a thrilling ride up one side of Mt. Penn and down the other, and a sweeping 30-mile view from the top of the mountain.

The building of the railroad on the mountain which forms Reading's eastern backdrop was part of a loose plan to develop Mt. Penn as a resort, similar to its sister hill, Neversink, which bounds the city to the south.

In the spring of 1889, construction started on the seven mile, standard gauge rail line which would ascend the western slope of the mountain, run along its crest and carry passengers on a 45-minute ride through woods, vineyards and meadows back to the station in the city's

Pendora Park section.

One of two 28-ton Shay locomotives would rumble two miles to the 1,200-foot summit of the mountain, and the rest of the journey would rely on gravity, controlled, of course, by the latest and safest braking apparatus. The cars would be released and sent on their way back to the depot.

That downhill stretch was negotiated at no faster than 12 miles per hour, and the last major turn on the winding way was on the sheer side of Dengler's Hill, at the southern tip of Mt. Penn.

That turn was known as the "hairpin turn" by the nature of its tight design, and as "cemetery curve," because it overlooked Aulenbach's Cemetery in East Reading.

On Friday, August 22, 1890, the latter monicker was to become all too prophetic as tragedy struck the fledgling rail excursion line, in its first full year of operation.

Charles Rettew had quit his job as conductor on the Wilmington and Northern Railroad to join the Gravity in a similar capacity. He was conductor for the morning runs that Friday.

In the 7:05 and 9:05 trips that day, all seemed well, except for one of the cars, No. 9, which had apparently hesitated when it reached Cemetery Curve during the 9:05 jaunt. The situation was not deemed critical, however, and the car was pressed into service again for the 10:05 trip.

Conductor Rettew manned his post, as did Frank Heller, the brakeman.

"The car had been inspected as all are before starting from the depot," Heller recalled. "When we had been pushed to the summit at the tower we tried to apply the brakes, but were unable to stop the car and it went down the gravity at an increasing speed."

Heller, who sustained internal injuries in the ensuing accident, was backed up by Cornelius Hanlon, a passenger on car No. 9.

Hanlon was a Reading Railroad engineer from suburban Philadelphia, and he and his wife decided to sample the Gravity Railroad ride on their way to visit friends in Pottsville. He had no idea what would happen that day.

"The accident was the worst I ever saw, although I have been railroading for a number of years," he said. "It is plain to everyone who knows anything about railroading that the engine left the car too quickly and that the car was running too fast. One of the chains broke and the other brakes were no good.

"I made a desperate attempt to stop the car when I saw the danger we were in, but when I found that the brakes were almost useless, I went into the car and told my wife of our peril. I wanted to take our children and jump, but my wife refused to leave the train.

"Believing that it was best to remain, we took seats on the floor in the rear of the car, holding the children. All the other passengers remained in their places, pale and trembling. The train must have been dashing down the road at the rate from 35 to 40 miles per hour!"

Other passengers concurred that the brakes had failed.

Howard Homan, another veteran railroader, said the problem was noticed as soon as the engine released the car at the Tower Hotel at the top of Mt. Penn. He said the crew of the car made a valid and valiant attempt to slow down or stop the car.

As No. 9 rolled faster from the summit, and it appeared that there were definite brake problems, brakeman Heller leaped from the car, and ran ahead hoping to purposely derail the car at a relatively flat area near Antietam Lake. The car beat him to the curve, and beyond that point was a winding, steadily dropping road which led to the infamous hairpin turn at the cemetery.

When Rettew saw that Heller had not made it to the curve at Antietam, he no doubt knew all was lost, and the runaway car was in the hands of fate.

As it descended along the straightaway which dropped on a 3.5 percent grade, the car rolled faster and faster. Two women, one with a baby in her arms, jumped from the car as it sped toward the hairpin turn. They were determined not to chance what they felt would be much more serious injury if the car derailed on the tight curve. They all survived with minor injuries.

Witnesses said there were no screams of panic on the runaway car. Passengers clung tightly to anything they could. They cowered under seats, and remained stoic through it all. There was little they could do but pray, hang on, and hope for the best.

It was a quiet kind of terror.

Those last few yards and moments, as Cemetery Curve came into view and the sheerness of the cliff just beyond it was realized, must have been moments of sheer horror for those aboard car No. 9 that Friday morning.

Up to the very end, every able-bodied railroader on the car made fruitless attempts to apply the hand brakes. At about 10:30, all was lost.

The car swept into the curve and almost immediately twirled from the track and tumbled some 70 feet. Trees snapped and the earth was chopped as the fragile, open-sided car caved in, rolled, came to rest upside down and its passengers were hurled into a mass.

When the wreckage finally settled, five people lay dead, and a score injured. Among the lifeless bodies pulled from the rubble was that of conductor Charles Rettew.

Rescue workers were at the scene almost immediately. What was left of the car was taken to the Gravity Railroad car barn on S. 19th Street, and the dead and injured were dispatched to morgues and hospitals.

Theories about the cause of the wreck and who was to blame were debated that day and well beyond, and while nobody wished to speak ill of the dead, many placed the blame directly on Charles Rettew, who had apparently made the final decision to again use the same car which had some evidence of a problem on the earlier run.

One railroader who survived the wreck said the two types of brakes on the car interfered with one another, and the air brake mechanism prevented the hand brake from working properly.

Company officials said they doubted that was the cause, but promised to investigate.

Car inspectors were quick to defend their actions prior to sending car No. 9 back up the hill after it had balked on the 9:05 run.

Joseph Monasmith said he rode both earlier runs, and had personally tested the hand brakes. They were working fine.

Tyson Hafer acknowledged that Rettew complained that the hand brake stuck on the 9:05, but after he looked into it, he pronounced both braking systems to be in good working order.

The railroad suspended operations the rest of that day, but as a coroner's jury was seated, the Gravity went back into service. On Saturday and Sunday, more than 2,700 passengers paid their quarters and dimes and took the ride. Some certainly came for the 30-mile view from the top or the fresh, lush fields and forests of the slopes of Mt. Penn. Others probably came for the morbid thrill of gazing upon the scarred embankment at Cemetery Curve.

After the wreck, certain additional safety precautions were taken, and only the hand brakes were used until mechanical investigations were completed.

The coroner's jury came to a fairly swift decision on the cause of and blame for the accident. The verdict stopped short of mentioning names, but was nonetheless to the point:

> *The fact that the 9:05 train stuck at the
> cemetery curve admonished all concerned
> that there was danger with the brakes. To
> put the blame on the conductor, or he with
> the brakeman, on the 10:05 a.m. train might*

be reasonable, but they should not bear the
responsibility in acting as the agents for
the company, which, it is admitted, employed
brakemen and car inspectors who knew
nothing about the brake lately adopted and
which had not stood the test of experience.

The Mt. Penn Gravity Railroad executives and employees had learned their lessons after the fatal wreck on Cemetery Curve that August.

Or had they?

On the afternoon of November 5, 1891, cars 1 and 10 careened off the tracks at another turn just south and west of Cemetery Curve. Two crewmen were killed, and the line immediately shut down for the rest of the season while safety factors were once again assessed.

That second accident resulted in sweeping changes to the right-of-way of the railroad. Runaway sidings and switchbacks were built to arrest any cars which would be speeding unabated toward dangerous curves. After those modifications were made, there was never again a serious accident on the Gravity.

Tens of thousands of riders used the line in the next two decades, until a series of events led to the demise of the mountainside railway.

First the novelty wore off as automobiles enabled folks to find their own ways into the hills and countryside for recreation and sightseeing.

Second, the observation tower atop Mt. Penn was destroyed in a fire which lit up the sky over Reading in April, 1923.

Its central attraction a charred ruin, and its uniqueness blunted, the Gravity Railroad's equipment was sold for scrap in the summer of 1924.

THE SHOEMAKERSVILLE WRECK
September 19, 1890

VICTIMS OF DEADLY TRAIN WRECKS WERE OFTEN AFFORDED DETAILED ENGRAVINGS OF THEIR LIKENESSES IN THE NEXT DAY'S NEWSPAPER. SIX OF THOSE WHO WERE KILLED IN THE WRECK ALONG THE SCHUYLKILL RIVER NORTH OF SHOEMAKERSVILLE, BERKS COUNTY, INCLUDED (CLOCKWISE FROM TOP LEFT) MICHAEL SOMERS, EDWARD J. FOX, MAIL AGENT AMANDUS GREENAWALD, MRS. FOX, DAVID ANSTOCK AND JAMES BECKER.

DEATH BY THE RIVER
September 19, 1890
Shoemakersville, Berks County

The last decade of the nineteenth century was particularly deadly on the rail lines of Berks County, and on the main line of the Reading.

The decade closed with the horrible Exeter Wreck of 1899, and opened with an almost equally tragic accident near Shoemakersville.

Both trains were carrying festive passengers returning to their homes from what had been a day of fun and excitement, and both trains would carry more than a score of these happy souls to eternity.

The decade was one of great growth for what was officially known as the Philadelphia & Reading Railway. There were faster trains, more trains, more passengers and more stations, and while all that added up to more revenue, it also was a calculation for calamity.

At precisely 5:42 p.m., on that fateful Saturday, the Pottsville Express was dispatched out of Reading. Aboard were hundreds of men, women and children who had converged on the city from such avents as the State Firemen's Convention in Chester and the Berks County Fair in Reading.

All were looking forward to the last, long stretch home to Schuylkill County on the swift and safe expres.

John White was at the throttle, with fireman James Templin and conductor Harry Logan. All were from

Pottsville. The baggage master was E.W. Logan, of Shenandoah.

The train was building up speed as it approached the Perry Straightaway, about two miles north of the Shoemakersville station. The main line hugged the shores of the Schuylkill River, rising some 20 feet above the river at what was known as Mervine's Hill.

Engineer White had no way of knowing would greet him as he guided the big locomotive around the long curve.

Earlier, two southbound coal trains had left the Perry station, just a bit farther north. The first, pulled by engine No. 347 and engineer A.B. Gehry, split as a coupling broke. Gehry backed up to retrieve the wayward cars.

Another coal train was dispatched from Perry twelve minutes after No. 347. That train, behind engine No. 921, continued down with no knowledge that the 347 was occupying the track. Engineer Gehry had his train just about underway when James Vail, at the controls of the 921, rolled into the rear of the first coal train, knocking an eight-wheeler coal car off the tracks, spilling much of its cargo on the other tracks.

As the passenger train completed the curve, and built speed to what one expert felt must have been close to 65 miles per hour. White doubtlessly looked up in horror as the wreckage of the two trains could be seen, far too close ahead to avert yet another collision. Later, it was determined that only about 90 seconds had transpired between the collision and the approach of the express. There was no time, it was felt, to place torpedo-style signals on the track as a warning, alerting engine crews with a loud, sharp, BANG!

Along that remote track, on the dark side of dusk, the Pottsville Express plowed into the timbers and coals which had spilled from the previous wreck. The force sent the engine of the passenger train reeling down the embankment and another 150 feet or so into he river.

Behind it, the tender, baggage car, mail car and three passenger cars struck the wrecked coal cars and followed in fatal plunges.

"The horrors of the scene of disaster are simply indescribable," was the testimony of one of the rescuers at the scent. "It will take the daylight of tomorrow to fully reveal the awful wreck and ruin wrought. The engine lies in the bottom of the river, whose waters are about five feet deep and the baggage, mail and passenger cars are also in the water."

Steam hissed and rose from the water as the estimated 150 passengers fought for their lives as the lights of the train were doused and all were forced to struggle in nearly pitch darkness.

Some managed to scramble from the wreck and find their way to Shoemakersville to summon help. Rescue crews in Reading were called, and by 10 o'clock, 300 workers were at the scene to render assistance. A man who lived close to the site of the wreck said the sound of the collision could be heard for miles, and was as loud as the report of a cannon.

The full extent of the tragedy was not known for quite some time, since most of the dead were trapped beneath the cars, on the muddy, grassy floor of the river.

One of the first bodies to be retrieved from the wreck proved to be a shock for the rescuers. It was that of arts patron, real estate magnate and reputed millionaire William Shomo, of Reading.

There was no saving Engineer White or the other members of the crew. White was one of the most experienced engineers on the Reading, and his body was found beneath the firebox of the engine. The corpse of mail agent George Greenawald was found well after midnight, floating downstream in the Schuylkill. The discovery of several empty mail bags from the river several hours later confirmed that Greenawald was in the midst of doing his job when the collision took place.

The recovery of the engineer's body was not

without the grisly details which often accompanied accounts of nineteenth-century railroad accidents. White's was the 22nd, and last body taken out of the wreck of the express. A worker saw the engineer's arm extending from beneath the locomotive. He grabbed the limb, as as the newspaper article stated, "to his horror, it came off, having been crushed and severed at the shoulder." White had also been decapitated, and his head was not found for another hour, wedged in the truck of the smoking car, several yards downstream.

The search for the bodies and aid to the injured continued throughout the night. Volunteers even manned rowboats in the river to search amid the debris for any signs of life.

The railroad's new "traveling electric light plant" was brought to the scene to aid in the salvage and rescue efforts, and by midnight, Berks County Coroner Dr. John J. Hoffman arrived to start his grim tasks. He told a reporter at the scene there was no doubt that the wreck was the most devastating ever on the Reading. That reporter, in turn, commented in the Reading Eagle the next day, "It is universally regretted here because that road has made a record for itself in not having a serious accident in all its history."

Something called tragic irony was riding that train that night. One of the passengers on the express was George R. Kaercher, general counsel for the railroad. He had been one of the prime forces in the company's prosecution of the Molly Maguires several years before. After its discovery around sunrise, his body was taken by special train to his waiting survivors in Pottsville.

As daylight broke, the full impact of the wreck and its human toll was sickening. Passenger cars were hoisted from the water and up the embankment. In them were clusters of corpses. Some were crushed and disfigured, others were untouched. In the latter cases, the victims had apparently drowned.

Brakeman Michael Gillen, of Philadelphia, was in

the middle section of the express when it struck the coal trains' debris. He later provided the most graphic details of the wreck:

I was sitting in the front end of the first ladies' car, talking with Judge Stephens of Pottstown...I felt a tremendous shock. Before I could jump to my feet there was another, and then looking out through the front end of the car I saw what appeared to be a coal train running into our train. For a moment I was too surprised to do anything. The window beside which I had been sitting was open, and I might have jumped out, but something seemed to warn me not to do it, and I verily believe had I done so I would have been killed.

As I again looked forward, I could see the forward cars of the train being knocked into the river and hear the sound of the crackling timber as they ground together like kindling wood. I saw the entire side of the smoking car, which was just ahead of mine, torn out, and then I turned my back, thinking that my last moment had come.

Many of the passengers in my car were screaming, and several of them had climbed half way out of the windows. I shouted to them to keep quiet, and the next instant our car was struck and upset down the bank, but was not overturned. Seeing there was no immediate danger for those in our car, I jumped out into the river, which was about five feet deep there, and worked my way to the forward part of the wreck.

In one of the wrecked cars, I don't known which one it was, I heard a man shouting for help. "I'm not caught and I'm not hurt, but I can't get out," he said. He was penned in the car like a rat in a box and the wood was blazing all about him. I secured a bucket and began throwing water on the fire, and I think the man was saved. I had to work alone for some time, although there was a crowd of

89

*people standing on the bank above the wreck to
whom I shouted to come and help me. They
refused, however, and it was some time before other
help arrived. I tried to learn where White, the
engineer, was, but he was pinned down under the
engine, and the water was so hot that we could not
get at him.*

*There were seven cars in the train, and five of
them went down the bank. The mail, express, parlor
and smoking cars were so badly mashed together
that I could not distinguish them apart, except the
latter, which stood with one-half in the water and at
right angles with the track from which it had been
thrown. Both sides had been torn away and many of
its occupants were killed or injured.*

*The two cars behind us, a day coach and a
Pullman car, had not left the track, except the front
truck of the former, and those occupying seats in
them received nothing more serious than a severe
shaking up.*

**Another survivor, John Sonon, spoke of the shock
of the crash:**

*I am the P & R flagman at Cressona, and
was on my way to that place. I was in the
smoking car. Suddenly there was a loud
crash and the car jumped down the
embankment. It seemed everything was
broken into splinters in the very part of
the car I was.*

*The car caught fire and I was afraid we
would all be burned. I crept away and the
flames gotinto a blaze a few minutes after
I crawled out. The daughter of Benjamin
Long, of Shoemakersville, reached me her
hand and pulled me off the wreck which
was in the water. She washed my face and
brought some men to help me. I tell you,*

90

*it was terrible. Everything was quiet at
first, then you could hear people cry and
groan.*

At 9:30 the following morning, a somber train
carrying 15 of the victims of the wreck made its way from
the scene to downown Reading, where coffins were
unloaded as police officers did their best to hold back the
hundreds of spectators. The streets of Reading were
cordoned off from the train depot to the Henninger
morgue as the curious strained for a glimpse of the
macabre procession.

In addition to the 22 killed, more than 30 others
were injured in the wreck. As the revolutionary, new,
transportable electric lights and the more traditional
bonfires were extinguished at daybreak, and as reporters
from a wide area sorted out their eyewitness accounts,
several interesting sidebars peppered the papers in
following days.

Particularly interesting is the story of four
individuals who died together in Schuylkill that night.

Mr. and Mrs. Edward Fox and Mr. and Mrs. J.E.
Fredericks, all of Schuylkill County, had long planned a
visit to their mutual friend, Frank Heffner, in Reading.

Heffner had been telling them of the wonders
offered on a ride on the Mount Penn Gravity Railroad,
and had urged them to come to Reading to experience the
mountaintop excursion.

Finally, the time had come for the two couples.
Both women knew of the Gravity's recent fatal accident,
and were leery of the ride. However, after dinner at the
Mansion House in Reading, all were assured that the
Gravity's safety had been beefed up, and the trip would
be quite harmless.

That Friday morning, they rose early and took a
ride on the Gravity Railroad. They spent some time
shopping in downtown Reading that day, and boarded
the express back home to Pottsville in the evening. Their

91

fears of the Gravity's safety were assuaged, but they would have no idea that the ride on the secure, dependable P & R would be their last.

Also out of the Shoemakersville wreck there came the fleeting story of one F.W. (or J.M. or J.W., depending on which account you read) Kershner, of Shoemakersville.

Kershner was found wandering around the wreckage, and was taken into police custody because they thought he was acting suspiciously. When arrested, officers found a cuff button in his possession. He was suspected of robbing the bodies of the victims of the crash.

Kershner spent about three hours in a lockup, but managed to make bail. He admitted at the time that he did take a cuff button from the ground and look at it, but did not rob any of the bodies, and never intended to steal it, or anything else. Any jewelry on his person was his own.

After several of his neighbors provided excellent character references, and after a hearing, it was determined there was no evidence to prove Kershner had intended to steal the piece of jewelry. A detective corroborated his story, and added that Kershner had performe valiant duties in the rescue and recovery efforts. The detective, one of hundreds who rushed to the scene at the behest of the rail company, also criticized the officer who jumped to conclusions when he saw Kershner with the cuff button.

Later, Coroner Hoffman attested to the fact that there appeared to be no jewelry missing from any of the bodies.

The Shoemakersville Wreck ended the life of N.C. Vanderslice, of Phoenixville, who was a Republican candidate for the state legislature. Far less significantly, it also marked the last time on a train for John Williams.

The New York man was riding in the Pullman car, and he survived the accident. But not a week earlier, he had also survived a fatal wreck on the B & O Railroad. No longer willing to press his luck, he nervously told witnesses that he would never again ride the rails.

The intrigue did not end when service on the main line was restored late Saturday morning. Parts of bodies were scattered across a wide area, and workers mopped up at the scene as an estimated 10,000 gawkers came to the scene in the hours which followed the accident.

But was it an accident?

A battery of inquiries and some revealing testimony followed what had been the most deadly wreck ever on the Reading.

Railroad observers and experts immediately rose to criticize the conduct of the crews on the coal trains. Based on documents submitted to probers, it was determined that a flagman would have had a good four minutes to dash only 200 yards to warn the oncoming express as it entered the site of the wreck.

The engineer of the first coal train, Gehry, said the crash which caused the coal cars to roll over was not at all violent, and his locomotive had proceeded all the way to the Shoemakersville station, where the express engine seemed to pass by his locomotive safely.

The fatal wreck occurred beyond the distant curve, and Gehry said he didn't know about it until brakeman Henry Kemp told him, "The express train is in the Schuylkill."

Vail, the engineer of the second downbound coal train, said his train was nearly stopped when it hit the caboose of the first train. There was little damage, but the force was just enough to upset the coal cars.

After several days of hearing testimony from survivors, crewmen and witnesses, the Coroner's Jury deterined that Kemp, the brakeman of the first train, was negligent when he did not deal swiftly with the collision of the coal trains and the oncoming express.

The 32-year old resident of Reynolds, Schuylkill County, was served with a warrant on September 26, and while he maintained his innocence, the blame for the wreck of the express was placed on his shoulders. He said there was not much he could have done, considering the timing and geography involved in the complex chain reaction.

In addition, the crews of both coal trains were suspended.

No matter who was to blame, and if indeed blame could have been placed on any one person, the wreck at Shoemakersville that day became a bloody smudge on a relatively clean record the Philadelphia and Reading Railway had compiled.

ADMISSION OF GUILT
June 25, 1892
Harrisburg, Dauphin County

Throughout this volume, there are tales of outright horror, sorrow, tragedy and travail. Some train wrecks are noteworthy solely for their human toll. Some are significant for their particular geographic location. Some figure prominently in the history, growth and development of railroads.

The following story straddles each of these criteria. A dozen people died in what was the first major train wreck in Harrisburg.

But one bit of information about this train wreck is particularly significant. Read on.

There was no moonlight that night, and a steady rainfall was drenching the Harrisburg area. Just after midnight, the crew of the Dillersville local jockeyed the switch engine around the yards at Union Station.

The freight was on the westbound track, and its conductor was within his bounds as he put his train together.

The Western Express, a two-section passenger train, had departed New York at 6:30, and Philadelphia at 9:20 the previous evening. The six-car first section was delayed several minutes in Philadelphia, and stopped at the Dock Street tower as the freight shifting continued.

Robert Brown, the flagman of that first section, made his way to the rear of the train to warn the engine crew of the second section, in case it entered the yard before the first section could depart.

That second section was running particularly heavy, with several Pullmans and a baggage express car. By the time it arrived in Lancaster, it was already 23 minutes behind schedule.

The freight finished its switching just before 1:00 a.m., and the first section of the Western Express was cleared to Union Station.

A whistle signal recalled Brown. He hadn't had a chance, or, he felt, a need to place torpedoes or flares on the track. As his train began to move, witnesses stopped, looked and listened in horror.

Roaring around a sharp curve was the second section, on a collision course with the first section. The inevitable was unavoidable. In the day coaches of both trains, most passengers were in various stages of sleep, totally unaware of what was about to take place.

With an ear-shattering crash, the second section thundered into the steel Pullman car at the rear end of the first section, shoving it through the three wooden day coaches in front of it.

It was a classic, and cataclysmic telescope collision.

Steam burst from the locomotive. The day coaches of the first section were reduced to rubble within seconds as the engine shoved the Pullman through them.

Caught between the Pullman of the first section and five surging Pullmans coupled to its tender, the locomotive of the second section had its smokestack ripped away and its firebox virtually destroyed.

Somehow, though, its cab survived intact. Inside were Hugh Kelly, engineer, and Harry Neill, fireman.

Flames began to crackle from the wreckage, but quick-acting crewmen and passengers doused them with buckets of water as the rain helped to extinguish them.

Passengers were literally sent flying in all directions when the trains collided. Some escaped with minor injuries, others were horribly mutilated, and when rescuers sorted through the shattered day coaches, they

96

looked upon scenes of sheer misery.

Chicagoan F.W. Heaney survived and helped in the rescue efforts. "I was in the smoker when the crash came," he said. "We were all thrown out of our seats and stunned for a moment. Right ahead of me was a man who I believe was a foreigner. A double seat caught him and the heavy stove fell on him also, breaking both legs. In trying to push off the stove it caught my hand.

"When I got out I saw a woman taken from the parlor car with her head crushed horribly. Other dead and injured were on every hand. I have been in wrecks before, but never saw so much damage in so short a time."

Several major industries, with night shifts working, found out about the wreck almost immediately. Employees poured from them to help. Soon, police, fire, and hospital workers arrived at Union Station. A temporary morgue was established in the station.

Crews worked through the night to clear the tracks, and it was not until 8 a.m. the next morning that Union Station was reopened to regular passenger service.

Pennsylvania Railroad Middle Division Superintendent O.E. McClellan coordinated the rescue, and the railroad's general manager, expressed his shock as the first theories of blame for the crash placed the responsibility on Hugh Kelly, engineer on the second section of the express.

"It is a terrible affair," G.M. Pugh said, "and I feel it all the more because the employees through whose fault it occurred were men in whom we had special confidence.

"Hugh Kelly, the engineer of the train that caused the accident, is one of our very best men, sober at all times, competent and a church member of the highest integrity. I know him personally, and knowing him as I do, I cannot understand how he could have failed to see the signal. It is incomprehensible to me."

Kelly's fireman on that trip also heaped praise on Kelly, and told investigators that he felt there was little the engineer could have done to prevent the collision.

While Kelly was arrested and later found guilty of not having his train under control as it entered the yards that night, the fault of the crash was not all his.

Fireman Neill of the second section, later testified that when that train reached Steelton, a white signal was displayed, and there were no torpedoes placed on the track.

The train was running about 35 miles per hour, and through the driving rain, the track ahead seemed to be clear. About 100 yards away from the rear of the first train, the red flag of danger was first noticed by the crew of the second section. It was too late.

At that point, engineer Kelly, a 21-year veteran of the Pennsy, whistled, reversed his engine and put his air brakes in emergency. Since a train of that consist would normally require 500 yards to stop, it was hopeless to expect the train to avoid a collision.

Kelly mentioned to the Coroner's Jury on June 28 that the Dock Street Tower in the yards had always been a source of confusion for engineers. One particular electric light on the Dock Street overpass tended to blind oncoming engineers, and in the rain that night, that light was especially distracting.

In the end, Kelly was punished, as was Robert Brown, the flagman of the first section. Brown was charged with not properly signalling the second section.

But the brunt of the responsibility for the wreck was borne by H.S. Hayes, the telegraph operator at the Steelton tower.

The 22-year old Hayes was found guilty of gross negligence for permitting the second section of the express to enter the block between Steelton and Dock Street, Harrisburg, before the first section had left. He was held on a criminal charge of manslaughter.

Described as an "unsophisticated youth" who had secured a job with the railroad after he left his family's farm in York County only a few months back, Hayes broke down when the verdict of the Coroner's Jury was

98

read.

Hayes had been assigned to a variety of posts as a relief worker on the Pennsy. On that fatal night he had drawn the trick on the Dock Street Tower as a substitute for regular operator William Good. During questioning after the wreck, Hayes admitted that he give the "all-clear" to the second section of the express without knowing that the first section was still in the block.

What's more, he confessed that two other unauthorized persons were in the tower with him at the time of the blunder, which was another violation of railroad regulations.

While the Harrisburg wreck was adjudged to be caused by negligence, and while even the most powerful air brakes would not have brought the heavy second section to a stop on 100 feet of wet track, there is a story within a story which should be told.

When the engine of the second section slammed into the Pullman car at the end of the first section, that Pullman was rammed through three wooden coaches in front of it. The engine was all but destroyed. The Pullman was virtually unscathed.

In that Pullman, a porter from Philadelphia was shaken up, but none of the other passengers was injured. The Pullman proved to be an island of safety in a sea of wreckage.

That Pullman was a special, private car, and in it was a man who had been almost single-handedly responsible for a development which made railroad trains far safer in the late nineteenth century.

For years, engineers and inventors had been searching for a swift, reliable braking system for trains. Safety on American railroads had deteriorated to the point that the media had begun to sit up and notice.

In his fine 1907 book, *Development of the Locomotive Engine,* Angus Sinclair wrote, "As long as vehicles continue to be run at high velocity, fatal accidents will be common from unavoidable causes such as the

99

breakage of material or human fallibility.

"Such accidents will be condoned; but others that result from absence of well-known safety appliances will always excite wrath and demands for punishment. The reluctance of railroad managers to adopt good brakes caused disasters too numerous to record, just as the reluctance of railroad companies to introduce proper train block systems is today making a sanguinary record."

Hand brakes could not contraol fast, heavy trains and ever larger, more powerful locomotives.

It came down to a New York man who, shortly after hitches with the army and the navy, decided to experiment with safety devices for the burgeoning railroad industry. In 1869, he introduced to a waiting nation the Straight Air atmospheric brake. After trying to persuade railroad officials that it would be effective, Westinghouse managed to have the brakes tested on the Pennsylvania Railroad. That line, and others after it, adopted the new braking system, and Westinghouse's fame and fortune was assured.

Fate dealt Westinghouse a fortunate card that night in Harrisburg. The last car in the first section of the Western Express was the private car of one George Westinghouse, Jr.. He and his party survived the brutal collision not necessarily because of the reliability of the air brake he had invented, but because of the strength of a sleeping car designed and built by another George named Pullman.

THE FLAT ROCK TUNNEL WRECK
October 24, 1892

SKETCH ARTISTS WERE QUICK TO THE SCENE OF THE COLLISION BETWEEN TWO TRAINS JUST NORTH OF THE FLAT ROCK TUNNEL IN PHILADELPHIA THAT AUTUMN MORNING. (TOP) THE LOCOMOTIVES LIE IN A TUMBLED MESS; (BOTTOM) A DETAIL OF THE TELESCOPED PASSENGER CARS.

DEATH AT THE END OF THE TUNNEL
October 24, 1892
Near Belmont Hills, Montgomery County

Not since the terrible wreck at the Camp Hill station had Philadelphians been subjected to news the magnitude of which hit the papers on that cool, crisp October morning.

For one penny, Philadelphia Inquirer readers gasped at the headline, "DOWN BRAKES TOO LATE TO STAY DEATH," and read on for the typically nineteenth-century gory details which would follow.

Charles Billig and a crew of five were in the Manayunk area for the first time. The usual territory for their coal-shuttling train was in the rich coal fields of Schuylkill County. Before that October morning, Billig had never come any farther south than Port Clinton.

Engine No. 538 had picked up 40 cars at Pencoyd and another five at Campbell's siding, and was deadheading the empty gondolas back north after unloading its cargo at Port Richmond. The freight was moving slowly on the northbound tracks through the Flat Rock Tunnel, rumbling along at what its engineer later estimated to be about fifteen miles per hour.

Trains still travel through the Flat Rock Tunnel. As of this writing, it is clearly visible on the south side of the Schuylkill Expressway near Manayunk. The highway is wedged on an elevation between the bore and the Schuykill River, and passes right by the Flat Rock.

In 1892, the area was much more remote and foreboding. A dirt road paralleled river and railroad, at the foot of a 30-foot embankment next to the tracks. Manayunk was not a section of the city of Philadelphia, but a fairly self-sufficient suburban town.

On the north side of the tunnel, the down tracks had been congested with freight cars for several weeks, and all rail traffic was using the northbound tracks.

The coal train was apparently on what was called a "layoff" schedule, in which the conductor, William Gerlacher, would use his best judgement deciding when the train would depart and continue on its course.

Philadelphia and Reading Railway officials would later confirm that the coal train had been handed orders at West Falls to wait at Pencoyd for a meet with Shamokin Express No. 2. Because the southbound track was blocked by freight cars, both the coal train and the express would have to use the northbound track.

Accordingly, the Shamokin Express was given orders at Bridgeport to switch to the northbound track and proceed toward its expected 9:30 a.m. arrival at Broad and Callowhill Streets in Philadelphia.

Behind the express was The Ariel, also known as Train No. 32, which was headed for Philadelphia from Harrisburg. That train consisted only of an engine and a private P & R Pullman car. In that car was George D. Whitcomb, superintendent of the Main Line Division.

Engineer Thomas Fitch, who had a spotless record in his years at throttles, was bringing the Shamokin Express past the Glen Rose Station and along the river toward the Flat Rock Tunnel at about 25 miles per hour. Since orders had come down from the dispatcher in Reading, he had no reason to believe anything untoward would happen, even though he was advised that between West Conshohocken and West Falls, all trains would be using one track.

103

James Berfield was a brakeman on the coal train:

*I probably saw the approach of the passenger
engine, as soon as those who were in the cab
with our engineer. I understood that we had a
clear track to Merion, and the sight of that
monster thundering down upon us caused my
heart to stand still.*

*The engines were not ten feet apart when I
muttered a prayer and leaped out toward the
dusty road at the foot of the embankment. I
was in the air when the crash came and the
noise was deafening. It seemed to me that the
heavens and the earth came together in a
mighty jar.*

Coal and coal dirt exploded into the air, shards of
wood and glass sprayed from the point of impact, and as
Berfield looked up from his position at the bottom of the
hill, he witnessed a gondola car flying over his head.

Flames sparked by hot coals spewing from the
firebox spread through the wrecked cars, and steam burst
from the engines, which were virtually molded together.

A fire broke out in the wreckage, and the
Manayunk Fire Department was quick on the scene to
extinguish the blaze. Their rapid response is credited with
saving the lives of many people who were trapped in the
debris, and would have been unable to escape any
oncoming flames.

One can only imagine the terror which shot
through all concerned when the crew of the coal train
came from the dark of the tunnel into the light of morning
only to look ahead a dangerously short distance and see
the big loco of the express bearing down on it.

The engineer, Billig, was idly chatting with
conductor Jacob Kilrain on the fireman's bench when he
was distracted not by that vision, but by the plaintive
whistle for down brakes aboard the approaching express.

Billig and Kilrain jumped for their lives when in a split second they realized that nothing could be done to prevent the inevitable. Billig survived the leap from the footboard, Kilrain did not. The body of the 36-year old Tamaqua man was found in the wooded area near the scene.

Fireman Bernard Gallagher also escaped by making a quick exit from the coal train. His was not as heroic.

Gallagher was sitting in the tender of the train, and the first he knew of the collision was as he went flying into the air when the two trains met. He received only minor injuries.

Thomas Maloney, a Philadelphia salesman, was headed home on the express:

> *I noticed that after passing Bridgeport the speed of the train was perceptibly increased and we were soon flying along at a high rate.*
>
> *I noticed nothing until we struck the curve and then I felt the whole car jarring and quivering with the grind of the brakes.*
>
> *Simultaneously came the crash. I saw the forward end of the smoker a mass of flying timbers, dust, broken glass and struggling human beings.*

And as the dust settled and the echo of the crash subsided, the moans of the dying could be heard above the crackling of the fire. Seven of those human beings lost their struggles.

The dead were all in the first coach of the express. As the locomotives met head-on, the passenger train, which was running at nearly twice the speed of the freight, reduced the coal train locomotive to a tangle of twisted and broken iron. Having inflicted that damage on its counterpart, the engine of the express shuddered and reared high above the tracks and came back to earth on its side with a wrenching thud.

Four empty coal cars, including the one Berfield watched soar over him, were propelled into the trees and onto the narrow dirt lane at the base of the embankment. Several gondolas filled with coal, spotted on the southbound track, were also smashed by the collision.

A Roxborough newspaper carrier, W.J. Dougan, was on his way to the bank when he learned of the crash. A liveryman in Manayunk stopped him and asked him to help him take a team to the wreck site to lend any assistance they could.

Dougan was one of the first to enter the remains of the coaches which had been telescoped.

The sight inside was terrible. The seats of the car and broken timbers were piled almost up to the ceiling of the car, while the groans of the dying and injured added an awful aspect to the scene.

A couple of seats above where the stove was located was the body of a woman. We had a hard time getting her body. When we lifted the stove off her the hot coals fell out over her clothing. As we were getting her out the seat next to where her body was lying fell over, disclosing the body of another woman. She was partly covered with debris.

The fatal injuries of those who did not survive the crash were gruesome. Their bodies were taken by wagon to the baggage room of the West Manayunk Station and then to Isaiah Ryan's funeral home in Manayunk. Large crowds gathered at his establishment to identify the bodies or simply gaze in macabre curiosity.

Trains from Philadelphia and Norristown on both the Reading and Pennsylvania roads brought spectators to Shawmont Station, across the river. From there, the people were ferried across the Schuylkill to the scene.

Among those who died that day was David S. Herr, a member of the Pennsylvania State Legislature.

Rep. Herr had also served as a city councilman and city treasurer in his native Harrisburg, and was a prominent member of the state Republican party.

Among those who survived was the pastor of the First Baptist Church in Phoenixville, Rev. J. Madison Hare. Ironically, he had discussed death and dying with his congregation just the previous evening, but as he said after the collision, "this is about the closest I ever got to it. Two women who were in the seat in front of me were killed before my eyes." His sermons on death would never be the same again.

There was another survivor who caught the attention of those reporters who covered the event. She was the widow of the late general counsel of the Reading Railroad. Her husband, George R. Kaercher, had been killed in the spectacular wreck near Shoemakersvile, Berks County, only two years prior to the Flat Rock Tunnel Wreck.

Another noteworthy passenger was Anthony Bonzano, father of the general superintendent of the Reading Railroad. The senior Bonzano was in the Pullman car, and escaped unscathed.

As the undertaker went about his business, some 100 laborers in wrecking crews worked throughout the morning to clear the scene of the disaster for the resumption of rail traffic along the busy main line. They labored through the day to repair tracks and load what was left of the engines and cars on flat cars for the repair shops in Reading. When night fell, gasoline torches were employed.

The crack of the collision had echoed against the hills in the area, and within minutes, neighbors gathered to see what they could see--and take what they could take.

About a quarter-ton of spare ribs was among the cargo in the baggage car. As the car was ripped to shreds, it spilled its meaty load, and much of the pork was purloined by those who descended upon the wreck scene.

So, too, for the contents of a large trunk of hosiery

107

and other assorted goods which were scattered over a wide area.

Police officers from Manayunk arrived shortly to maintain order and ensure that the passengers' baggage would not fall prey to the scavengers. Special officers, including Reading Police Chief Richard Whitman, also helped in the railroad's efforts to secure the wreck scene and carry out investigations.

Still, the souvenir-gathering continued for many more days, as folks picked their way along the tracks and the embankment for any bits and pieces from the wreck.

In the meantime, P & R investigators sought the cause of the accident.

On November 4, Special Officer Peter E. Burns knocked on the West Manayunk door of John R. Rupp, who had been the yardmaster at the Falls of the Schuylkill yards of the Reading the day of the Flat Rock Wreck. The officer informed Rupp that the Coroner's Jury had charged him with negligence, and with the ultimate responsibility for the crash.

The coroner's jury met in the offices of the Ashland Paper Mills in West Manayunk, which proved to be too small to accommodate the parade of witnesses and crowd of spectators. Thus, most people were forced to wait outside until it was their turn to testify.

There was much tension in the gathering, and some controversy, as well. There were vague rumors that both the railroad and private parties had made certain threats against the jury members.

Jury Foreman Perry L. Anderson made a cryptic statement before testimony began:

> *Now, people may pooh-pooh and pooh-pooh*
> *as much as they like, but I for one am not to*
> *be intimidated, whether the intimidation*
> *comes from the dignitaries of the Reading*
> *Railroad or their subordinates. How are we*
> *to fulfill the obligations of our oaths and*
> *diligently inquire into the causes of this*

accident if we do not consume ample time
in doing so, and we intend to take ample
time, be it ten hours, ten days or six months.

While the railroad was criticized for allowing inexperienced men to work on the main line, the blame was placed squarely on Rupp's shoulders for, as the findings said, "disobeying order No. 54 from Reading," which called for any northbound trains to be held up until the express passed.

Rupp's defense was simple. He asserted that he had authority of the traffic between West Manayunk and West Falls (Falls of the Schuylkill), no matter what the Reading office said. The jury didn't accept his claim.

Whether it was mere coincidence, or the fulfillment of the dreaded railroaders' superstition, the Flat Rock Tunnel Wreck was one of three which were in the headlines of area papers that week.

But even more significant was another story which broke as the news stories of the Flat Rock Tunnel Wreck were swept off the front pages.

That story warned of a "Monster Strike" of railroad employees in 1893. Already in the autumn of '92, spot walkouts on wage and manpower issues were being ordered by the Switchmen's Union, and other labor organizations were expected to follow suit.

This dispute between the railroads and their increasingly disgruntled employees would translate to tragedy for the rail-riding public.

THE FLAMES OF UNREST
December, 1893
White Haven, Carbon County
Easton, Northampton County
Fairview, Luzerne County

Sure enough, with 1893 came widespread labor unrest in America's railroad industry. In Eastern Pennsylvania, that year's end brought misery and destruction, particularly on the lines of the embattled Lehigh Valley Railroad.

On November 18, the executive officers of the railroad were informed that engineers, conductors, firemen, telegraphers and brakemen would walk off the job at midnight that night.

The various trades' committees handed down their intention, and the railroad refused to deal with the organized bodies. A month before, the railroad management was asked to consider certain complaints from employees regarding wages and hours, but nothing, the committees maintained, was done. The company said it would listen to the grievances of individuals, but not to the committees. About half of the 2,500 employees of the L.V.R.R. were organized in the committees at the time.

On that appointed strike day, workers did not wait until midnight. By 10 p.m. that night, those men represented by the committees simply, and quietly, walked off their jobs.

As the entire length and breadth of the Lehigh Valley was effectively shut down, company officials took swift action to hire non-organized workers to fill the positions of those who had gone on strike.

This move was the fanning of the flames of unrest which prevailed for a short but bitter time.

Those flames, both literally and figuratively, spread like wildfire throughout the Lehigh Valley Railroad system.

The usually quiet town of White Haven, on the edge of the Pocono Mountains, was nearly destroyed as the result of the careless acts of non-union workers, and throughout the Lehigh Valley and beyond, other more wanton acts of vandalism and malice took lives, destroyed property and cost the railroad enormous sums of money.

As wrecks said to be the direct result of inexperienced "scabs" swept the region, strikers stood solidly behind their cause. At the highest level of the railroad, a growing concern was building that middle-level management was hiring incompetent workers to replace the union men.

There were calls from the public and politicians for the railroad executives to do all they could to end the strike, but both sides remained steadfast as conditions on the line grew worse as November ended and December took its bow.

From Sayre, on the Pennsylvania-New York line, to White Haven and beyond, the L.V.R.R. was crippled by wrecks. At one time, the main line of the railroad was blocked for about 200 miles because of derailments and wrecks.

Passenger trains were running as many as five hours late, if at all. Miners and collieries throughout the coal regions were affected, as the valuable shipping of "black diamonds" was at a near standstill.

A suspicious "accident" took place near the roundhouse in the southeastern yards at Easton on December 2. There were no injuries, but the incident sent

111

a clear message to all concerned in the strike action.

The No. 300, also known as "The Dorothy," was the private engine of Lehigh Valley Superintendent E.P. Wilbur. During the strike, it was pressed into service by dispatchers.

That morning, the Dorothy was in Phillipsburg, N.J., its engineer and fireman minding their own business and trying to cope with the tension all around them.

Along the Easton and Amboy Division, Engine No. 192 was bound to lend assistance at a wreck site in Bloomsbury, N.J. Along the way, the engine, following close behind a coal train, collided with that train's caboose, demolishing it and several coal cars.

Upon impact, the engineer of the 192 reversed his engines and sped at an estimated 60 miles per hour toward Phillipsburg.

The unsuspecting crew on board the Dorothy looked up as the 192 was rolling directly toward them. The crewmen leaped from both engines as the 300 and the 192 collided. The forward motion of the 192 shoved the Dorothy through Phillipsburg, across the Delaware River Bridge, and past the Easton Station. There was no one in the careening locomotives. Anyone who witnessed the incident must have been a bit confused by it all as the paired engines roared along unattended.

As the runaway tandem entered the Easton yards, they bore down on yet another engine--that of an eastbound coal train. The big coaler was virtually immovable. The wild ride ended with the private engine crushed between the two freight engines.

Two brakemen who were inside the caboose of a coal train taking on water at Gracedale were killed when another freight train crashed into it and set the caboose on fire.

Near Avoca, in the rich coal country, the uncertainty of the labor situation caused a wreck near the Florence Colliery. The yardmaster, aboard a heavy coal train negotiating a long grade, felt the non-union engineer

112

could not adequately guide the train up the side of the hill, and he assumed control of the throttle.

He must not have seen the red signal at the colliery. Running at a good speed, the Lehigh Valley coaler slammed into the midst of a Delaware and Hudson freighter which was just pulling out. There were no injuries.

Another wreck in Fairview proved fatal for a crewman, and in its wake, two non-union workers were arrested for manslaughter.

Perhaps the most dramatic story came out of White Haven that same day, however, as the railroad strike grew even more deadly.

It was the middle of the night in White Haven when a heavy coal and freight train lumbered down the main line, on a long grade which flattens out at the edge of town. As the engineer, an inexperienced, non-union man, reached that flat stretch, he built up steam, forgetting to release his brakes. The train split into two sections.

Unaware that his train had split, or unable to do anything about it, the engineer continued at top speed, and through White Haven, the second section rolling close behind. That section eventually came to a stop in the middle of the town.

A brakeman on the isolated section left the caboose to flag any trains which may be approaching from the rear. He was assuming a position farther up the tracks when he saw big engine 171 rounding the bend and coming down the grade at about 50 miles per hour.

The brakeman knew, and the engineer of the 171 knew, that the long freight train could not be stopped.

The oncoming freighter crashed into the crippled train, and the caboose and several other cars laden with grain burst into flames as the 171 was shattered by the impact.

The crash took place only yards from the Ruhnke Hotel, and propelled by a stiff wind that early morning, the flames licked the frame building until the hotel became fully involved in the blaze.

The merciless wind then spread to Ricker's General Store, and then to a stable, Drigg's drug store and hotel, Smith's Hotel, two shops and several homes.

As the residents of White Haven were rudely awakened by the roar of the collision, they rushed to the scene to save their town.

Fire fighters, including volunteers from the ranks of the striking railroaders, managed to contain the fire, and by dawn the wind shifted away from the town buildings and the threat of further destruction was eased.

Because of the nature of the day, the railroad sent representatives from management to help in the aftermath of the fire, and also hired armed deputies to patrol the tracks near the scene.

When the sun rose that morning, one full block of White Haven was nothing but charred ruin, and three railroad men were missing within it.

The rubble was not yet cold when the railroad issued a statement which accused striking workers of pulling pins of the freight train and causing the accident. That charge further infuriated an already seething workforce.

Random acts of sabotage and vandalism were reported throughout the region, and as an indication of how bad the situation was, even the wrecking train which was returning from White Haven to Hazleton was itself wrecked when it collided with a freight train at Glen Summit. Inexperienced workers were again blamed.

These were the darkest hours of the strike on the Lehigh Valley in late 1893. They were also the hours, and the incidents, which broke the artibrators' backs.

The labor dispute had already been turned over to arbitration boards in New York and New Jersey, and on December 6, a communique issued to the president of the Lehigh Valley R.R. in South Bethlehem advised him that the strikers would return to work if they would be assured of their jobs and would would face no recriminations as the result of the strike.

That final action and agreement came, it was reported, with no small token of gratitude to Mary Cummings, one of the richest women in the world and the daughter of Mauch Chunk millionaire Judge Asa Packer, who had established the Lehigh Valley Railroad.

Watching the equipment, the morale, and the reputation of the railroad fall, Mrs. Cummings quietly but firmly urged an end to the violence. She apparently called for sweeping company concessions, and the resignation of its president.

Indeed, pay raises promised in the summer were granted, and working conditions were to be assessed, and improvements made when possible. The "scabs" were discharged, and the strikers were re-hired.

And, while the Lehigh Valley Railroad picked itself up by its bootstraps, White Haven struggled to rebuild and families throughout northeastern Pennsylvania planned and attended the funerals of those lost in a seemingly senseless reign of terror on the rails of Eastern Pennsylvania.

A WARNING FROM MOM
May, 1894

AS ENGINEER MILTON MOSER SPED BY AT THE THROTTLE OF THE EMPIRE LINE, THROUGH THE QUAKAKE VALLEY, HE PASSED HIS CHILDHOOD HOME. WITH FOUR SONS ON THE CREW THAT DAY, MOM AND POP MOSER WATCHED ANXIOUSLY AS THE TRAIN PASSED THEIR HOUSE. IN THIS ILLUSTRATION FROM *RAILROAD MAGAZINE,* MOM MOSER IS SEEN GIVING A SIGNAL OF WARNING TO HER SONS THAT THEIR ENGINE WAS FOLLOWING TOO CLOSE BEHIND ANOTHER TRAIN. MOMENTS LATER, THE EMPIRE LINE COLLIDED WITH THAT TRAIN, BUT THANKFULLY, THERE WERE NO CASUALTIES.

THE MOM AND POP WRECK
May, 1894
Quakake Valley, Schuylkill County

This story will serve as a breather from the wholesale death and destruction of the preceding (and proceeding) pages. It is a rather unique tale of togetherness, good fortune and a lot of luck.

H.O. Moser told the story in a 1948 issue of *Railroad Magazine.* His father was a railroader 51 years, a full four decades as engineer on the Lehigh Valley, and 17 of those years at the throttles of passenger engines. His grandfather was a railroader, his five uncles were engineers, and his two sisters were married to engineers.

It was a proud railroading family.

Moser recounted a story his father had told many times, about his narrow escape while bringing the Empire Line engine No. 547 through the picturesque valleys between Packerton, near Mauch Chunk, to Mount Carmel.

The mixed-freight Empire was run at top speed, and in two sections along that stretch. On the fateful morning in May, the elder Moser took the 15-car second section.

The Hazleton-built Clark engine "could run like a scared jack rabbit," according to Milton Moser.

The westbound run out of Packerton departed

117

the main line at Penn Haven, and joined the Mahanoy Division. The first ten miles of that link were a bit tricky, but at Black Creek Junction, the way opened up to 16 virtually straight miles in the Quakake Valley.

It was sit back, light up your pipe and open up time for the Empire, as the engine sped along at up to 50 miles per hour. For Engineer Moser, it was also a homecoming of sorts.

He had been brought up in the Quakake Valley, and in it was his old homestead where his parents still lived. Each time he brought a train through the valley, he would turn his attention to the old house along the tracks and return a wave from his mom and dad.

That morning, for that crew, would be especially poignant. Moser's fireman was his son-in-law, the brakemen were his younger brothers, and an older brother was firing.

As the train approached a cross-over where the tracks climb a steep grade and wind around several mountainside curves toward Delano, Moser looked forward to seeing his parents as he sped by.

At one of the curves, Moser glanced ahead and thought he saw puffs of smoke rise above the trees. He knew the first section of the Empire was at least ten miles ahead, and when the conductor said he saw nothing, Moser dismissed the fleeting fear that the smoke might have been coming from the first section, which would have been unusually close.

After maneuvering around the curves, Moser positioned himself in the back of the cab with his brothers and awaited the pass of their old home.

Sure enough, as they rolled past, Moser's parents were on the side porch to greet them with a wave.

This time, however, it was not a wave of welcome.

His mother firmly lifted her arms straight to the sky, and with hands straightened, moved her arms together, then open, then together again.

It was a signal known to engineers that another

train was dangerously close ahead.

Just past his parents' house, the tracks curved again into a blind spot. Moser knew what to do, and began to swing into action. But as his engine came out of the curve, he saw the trainman's worst fear. Ahead of him, far too close to avoid, was the first section of the Empire Line. Its flagman was frantically waving the red flag, knowing as well that it was too late.

"Jump, boys!," screamed Moser, and the crewmen obeyed. He reversed the lever, hit the steam brake, and leaped from the cab to the tender and into a ditch.

The 547 crashed into the caboose of the first section, and the sound rattled in the valley. The engine telescoped the caboose into freight cars of the first section, and rolled down a steep and deep embankment.

Right into the back yard of Moser's sister-in-law.

She was working in the kitchen when she heard the crash. She ran to the back door and saw the big engine tumbling into her yard.

Meanwhile, back at Moser's parents' house, the sound of the crash had panicked the engineer's mother and father. Both were certain their boys must have been killed in the collision.

They were not, and in fact the 547 was retrieved from the bottom of the embankment and lived to roll again, with Milt Moser at the throttle.

THE EXETER WRECK
May 12, 1899

CONTEMPORARY ENGRAVINGS DEPICT THE SCENE NEAR WHAT IS NOW LORANE, BERKS COUNTY, IN THE AFTERMATH OF A WRECK WHICH KILLED 29 PERSONS. UP TO THE TIME OF WHAT BECAME KNOWN AS "THE EXETER WRECK," IT WAS THE WORST EVER DISASTER ON THE PHILADELPHIA AND READING RAILROAD. (TOP) GUARDS MAINTAIN ORDER WHILE RESCUERS SEARCH FOR THE INJURED AND DEAD; (BOTTOM) A DEPICTION OF ENGINE 574, WHICH WAS PULLING THE SECOND SECTION OF A SPECIAL TRAIN.

THE EXETER WRECK
May 12, 1899
Lorane, Berks County

It was the most devastating train wreck in the history of the once-mighty Reading Railroad, and it remains as one of the most stirring tales of railroad terror in the annals of Eastern Pennsylvania.

It was Friday night, May 12, 1899. Just before nine o'clock, a train rumbled along the rails from Reading to Philadelphia. The scheduled "down express" was made up of express and baggage cars, day coaches and a Pullman.

Dubbed the "Cannon Ball Express," the train had pulled out of Reading's Outer Station about ten minutes behind schedule.

A scant six minutes after the express chugged out of that main terminal, another train was dispatched from Reading.

Technically, it was the second section of Train No. 12, which included the Cannon Ball Express. That "second section" of No. 12 was a special run, filled with passengers returning to Norristown after their participation in the dedication of a monument in Harrisburg. They included mostly veterans, firemen, musicians and dignitaries returning from what had been a happy day in the capital.

They were in Harrisburg for the unveiling of a monument to Civil War General (and later Pennsylvania governor) John Hartranft. Many of them were members of the G.A.R. post in Norristown, the Montgomery Hose Co., the 51st Regiment Band, and several had served under Gen. Hartranft in the war.

The firemen from Norristown were well known to many Readingites. Just months before, they had been the guests of the Rainbow Fire Co. at the State Firemen's Convention.

As the regularly-scheduled train coasted past the Exeter Station (known now as Lorane), it came to a stop. A northbound coal train was experiencing problems with its brake rigging a few miles down the line in Birdsboro. The express was in the process of backing up to the station siding.

About a mile up the tracks, the special train was speeding south at what one observer felt was nearly 50 miles per hour. There was a party atmosphere on board as the revelers were just minutes away from their homes.

The tracks were dark that Friday night, and all seemed well as Engine 574 sped south past Neversink , through a long straightaway, and around a gentle curve toward Exeter Station.

As the signal lantern at Exeter came into view, Engineer Harry Orrell knew tragedy was about to strike.

"I was horrified to see loom up a few hundred yards ahead, the first section," Orrell later told a reporter. "I instantly put on the brakes, opened the sand box and reversed the lever, but before I could stop the engine, we went into the rear of the train ahead with a terrible crash.

"My engine ploughed through the day coach, which in turn crashed halfway through the Pullman Porter car. The impetus of the collision sent the parlor car halfway through the day coach in front of it."

Orrell's recollections of his moment of terror grew more intense. "I did not know where I was for a time, but finally discovered myself imprisoned among twisted trees, splintered wood and broken glass. I got out of the wreck unaided. How I escaped without more serious injury I cannot tell."

Engineer Orrell was one of the fortunate ones.

The roar of the crash was deafening. John Esterly was at his house more than a mile away, along the Perkiomen Turnpike (now Route 422), when he heard a sound he described as "the muffled falling of a great building or the simultaneous descent of a dozen trees in the forest."

It was the Exeter Wreck.

The most chilling eyewitness account of the crash came from William K. Lutz, the proprietor of the Exeter Station Hotel.

Lutz, and Exeter residents James Toal, Jonathan Gerhart and Francis Sweitzer were mulling about the station that night when they noticed the unusual but not unheard of sound of the first section of Train No. 12 coming to a halt at the station.

The men ambled onto the platform of the station, only to witness with great anguish the second section, pulled by Engine 574, rounding the curve to their right.

"We waited for the crash, which we knew must come," said Lutz.

"I saw sparks fly from the wheels of the second train as the air brakes were applied," he continued. "I saw Charlie Miller, the hind man of the first section, run back with his lantern at the top of his speed. He continued swinging it until the second section was within 15 feet of him.

"I thought he was running an immense risk and it was certainly brave of him to stand there with every probability of having the wreckage thrown upon him. But the time between the two trains was just too short."

There was no fire, just the gut-wrenching, monstrous roar of the giant Wootten engine smashing into the cars of the halted express.

"God certainly bestowed a blessing upon us all through the absence of fire," said survivor Filmore Jones of Norristown. "Several times, small flames broke out, but were quickly subdued," he added.

Only through horrific hindsight can one imagine the human and property toll which would have been exacted if an explosion or fire had been added to the impact of the collision.

That prospect notwithstanding, the carnage which followed in the wake of the crash was unspeakable.

John Mayer, survivor and employee of the U.S. Mint in Philadelphia, was passing between cars of the special train when, as he later related, "I heard a succession of heavy reports like the noise of a cannon."

Mayer, who was also a former police sergeant in Norristown, continued. "I was violently thrown forward. I crouched down between the seats, expecting that the car would be thrown over. I got out by the door to walk back, but was obliged to pick my way through a lot of timbers and debris from the two wrecked cars in back of us."

Another man who escaped death was John Shaner. His recollections of the crash were vivid. "It was positively the most terrible scene I ever looked upon," said the Pottstown resident. "The wreck was indescribable. Human arms and limbs sticking out of windows with splinters of wood driven through them; dead bodies piled in and around the wreckage; it was sickening."

Those who witnessed the crash provided more grisly details. The first two coaches of the second train were "ground into matchwood," said one unidentified spectator. Another anonymous witness recalled, "I saw a number of shapeless masses of humanity, several having their heads torn from their shoulders."

Catharine Gallagher, who was returning from Pottsville to Philadelphia aboard the express, gave a fascinating account of the crash.

"I was seated about the center of the coach, and the first intimation we received of the danger was when the air brakes were suddenly applied and the car gave a lurch. Before anyone had time to turn around, an awful crash was heard, followed by heart-rending screams from several persons seated behind me.

"I lost consciousness for a moment, but after discovering that, aside from a few body bruises, I was not hurt I made an effort to escape. I turned to get out by the rear end of the coach. But to my horror, I found that the front of the parlor car had cut its way clear through that section as far up as the seat directly in back of me.

"Our car was practically demolished, and the excitement that prevailed made it impossible to ascertain at the time of leaving the number of fatalities. There were several persons sitting back of me who were either killed outright or dreadfully mangled, as that portion of the coach was smashed by the collision.

"The moans of the dying and the cries of the injured were pitiful to hear as some of them were pinned beneath debris in such a manner as to make their rescue doubtful. It was necessary to clear the door of our coach of wreckage before any of the passengers could get out."

After watching what he knew was inevitable, William Lutz, the Exeter Station operator, instinctively swung into action.

The station became a field hospital for some, a morgue for others.

And, while the Exeter Wreck represented in many ways an example of railroading's darkest hour, it could also be remembered as one of its finest hours.

Lutz, his wife and daughter, Sallie, immediately embarked on a rescue mission which would have them in constant action for the next two exhausting days.

The rooms on the first floor of the hotel-station were filled with the dead and wounded. Every ounce of food, drink and medical supplies was gone within two hours of the accident. Every quilt, blanket, sheet, towel and necessary household item was removed from the hotel and family living quarters and pressed into service. Sallie even retrieved some of her old dresses to use for bandages.

Coaches which had survived the crash undamaged were also used as havens for triage operations. William Sullivan, a marble dealer, told of men who worked

125

throughout the chilly night stripped to their waists, their shirts and undergarments used as bandages.

Even though some passengers were pulled out of the wreck still alive, they died in the hotel and on its front porch despite the most valiant efforts of the rescuers to sae them.

Help was summoned, but was slow to arrive. Mary Moyer, who lived down the street from the station, was one of the first to render assistance by bringing quilts and cloth for dressings. By midnight, Mahlon Stitzer arrived from the nearby village of Gibraltar with food, and farmers from the area provided wreck crew members with provisions as the cleanup operations proceeded overnight and into the next two days and nights.

Doctors, nurses, druggists, emergency crews and undertakers rushed to Exeter Station after word reached Reading some 30 minutes after the collision. The first train to arrive at Exeter after the call for assistance took seven doctors to the scene.

It was a busy Friday night in the city, some seven miles away. Pedestrians along Penn Street suspected something was awry along the rails when the Pennsylvania and Reading Railroad wreck train sped south from the yards, and the Reading Hospital ambulance made its way hastily up Penn Street.

Crowds gathered at the 7th and Penn Streets track crossing and speculation mounted that tragedy had struck somewhere south of the city.

Private wagons, teams and barouches were called to serve as impromptu ambulances, and the roads to Exeter were rapidly crowding with those who responded to the unprecedented call for aid. Images of a similar call nine years back, when 22 passengers died at a train wreck near Shoemakersville, north of the city, came to the minds of many.

Soon, the tentative confirmation of a deadly train wreck sent the curious scrambling aboard southbound coal and freight trains which were about to depart the

126

Reading yards.

The attempts of these morbid thrill-seekers were foiled within minutes when all rail traffic was halted by dispatchers.

Reporters from the Reading Eagle also scrambled to the scene quickly. While railroad officials denied the newsmen access to special wreck trains, the determined scribes hired their own carriages and made their way down the Perkiomen Turnpike to the remote Exeter Station.

What they found at the wreck site became fodder for a gory first-hand account.

It was about three o'clock in the morning when the unidentified writer managed to make his way to the tracks at Exeter. The resulting newspaper story was graphic.

"One of the first things to come under the reporter's gaze," the article began, "was a rather tall looking man, pinioned by the roof of the passenger car, and lying at full length on his side on the steaming boiler, where he had slowly roasted to death."

The newspaper pulled no punches in its descriptions of the injuries which led to the deaths of 29 and the serious injuries of more than four dozen more passengers.

"E.E. Sheeley, Hatboro...head badly crushed..."

"Charles Howell, Phoenixville...skull crushed..."

"An unknown man...dismembered...a number of his ribs and right hip bone protruted...his head was almost severed from his body and was crushed into a pulp..."

That last unknown corpse was the last to be removed from the wreckage, at about 4:30 a.m., some seven hours after the crash. His remains were removed later that morning to a Reading funeral home.

The mortuaries of the city were all kept open throughout the long night of May 12, as the bodies arrived by coach and wagon.

The Theodore C. Auman morgue filled rapidly.

Among the fatalities taken there was Daniel H. Yoder, whose legacy proved to be an interesting sidebar.

The 36-year old widower was a native of Boyertown, Berks County. He had been living in Pottstown and was returning home from a visit with his sister on Cotton Street in Reading. While in Reading, Yoder had also attended the grand opening of the Hotel George in center-city and had responded to a job offer at a city marble fabrication plant.

Yoder's children, who ranged in age from 3 to 16, had accompanied him to Reading and were due to return with him on the train that night.

The children, who were visiting their aunt and uncle in Reading, begged their father to extend their stay, and after considerable discussion, Mr. Yoder relented. The children stayed behind, and would join their father in Boyertown on a later train.

It was never to happen. And, had he not given in to their pleas, they may very well have been killed along with him.

The victims of the Exeter Wreck of 1899 were young and old, male and female, and from all walks and stations of life.

"Joseph Taylor, a colored porter...almost crushed into a shapeless mass..."

"Frank D. Bower...one of the best known and highly-respected businessmen of Norristown..."

"Captain George W. Schall...the ex-postmaster and burgess (mayor) of Norristown..."

"John C. Slingluff...chief of the Norristown Fire Dept., president of Montgomery National Bank, treasurer of the State Fireman's Assn., prison inspector...pinned in the debris, strangling him to death..."

Slingluff's death provided a touching vignette within the horrid wreck story. As his body was carried onto the station platform, an unidentified young survivor relentlessly patted the lifeless form on his forehead. "With tears streaming from his cheeks," a later news article

THE EXETER WRECK

JOHN C. KUNTZ,
NORRISTOWN.

WILLIAM STAHLER
NORRISTOWN

CAPT. E.T. STREET,
PHILADELPHIA.

WILLIAM LEWIS,
NORRISTOWN

CHAS. H. C. WHITE,
NORRISTOWN,

JOHN RESSGUFF

H.H. THOMPSON,
NORRISTOWN

COLONEL GEO. SCHALL
NORRISTOWN.

ISAAC FILMAN,
NORRISTOWN

NORMAN HOLMES,
THE YOUNGEST VICTIM.

LUCIEN CUSTER,
POTTSTOWN.

H. C. WENTZ,
NORRISTOWN.

VICTIMS OF THE EXETER WRECK OF MAY 12, 1899 INCLUDED YOUNG AND OLD. THE READING WEEKLY
EAGLE PUBLISHED PORTRAITS OF SOME OF THE VICTIMS IN ITS EDITION PUBLISHED AFTER THE WRECK.

began, "the young man exclaimed, 'he was the best friend I had in the world! Oh, this is terrible!'"

Slingluff's body was found by Peter Hoy and Henry Pagel, who were seated just behind the fire chief. After the crash, they struggled in the wreckage of the car to see if anyone else in it was alive. With only the flickering light of a match, they stumbled into Slingluff's lifeless body. They managed to remove his body by wrapping it with pieces of the whistle cord, throwing the end of the cord to rescuers positioned on top of the overturned car, and easing it out of a window as they pulled from above.

The borough of Norristown was devastated by the news of the loss of so many of their own, be they prominent leaders or common citizens.

The Philadelphia Public Ledger offered a touching editorial, which linked the festivities in Harrisburg with the tragedy in Exeter.

> *It was Norristown that gave to the state and county Hartranft; within the borough's borders rest his remains; here his memory is cherished as it can be cherished in no other community.*
>
> *That the town who knew and loved him best should suffer a loss as was inflicted when its proud sons were returning to their homes, after honoring that idol of the populace, seems as strange as it is dreadful.*

The borough council called a town meeting the day after the wreck, and the victims were given brief eulogies. A resolution passed by council expressed its deepest sentiments. "This accident, so appalling in its suddenness, so terrible in its immediate results and so heart rending in its wide spread of sorrow, has prostrated our town with lamentation and mourning," it read. "The news in the night of yesterday brought greater desolation to our community than ever came to it any one time from the battles of four wars," it concluded.

Two days after the wreck, Gov. Hartranft's widow and her daughter, Marion and son, Linn, issued their expressions of grief, and set out to visit as many of the survivors and victims' families as they could.

When the dust settled after the crash, more incredible tales of both death and salvation emerged in the Reading press.

It was discovered that U.S. Senator Boise Penrose was aboard the "Cannon Ball Express," and his survival hinged on a fortuitous move made in Reading.

"I rode from Harrisburg to Reading in the rear of the parlor car," he said, "but at Reading I got off to obtain some lunch. Instead of returning to my place in the parlor car, I took a seat in the smoking car, which was at the extreme forward of the train. That was a lucky move, because if I had gone back to my old place I undoubtedly would have received some sort of injury."

Also among those who escaped with their lives was Prof. Joseph Remington, the dean of the Philadelphia College of Pharmacy.

The newspapers in Reading, Norristown and Philadelphia started asking questions about the cause of the crash even as the ebris from the catastrophe was still being cleared.

That cleanup of the scene was no easy task. Two day coaches and a parlor car were demolished so completely that they were shoved over an embankment and burned. Scavengers were on the scene like vultures, picking out ornate mirrors and plush seats from the parlor car, and scouring the scene for relics and souvenirs.

In fact, widespread reports claimed that "ghouls," as they were called, were also at work at the wreck. There was talk of missing jewelry, watches, and pockets of the dead turned inside out, allegedly by local residents and even uniformed guards.

Major Henry Pennington, a passenger on the first section, said he saw the plundering. His story was backed up by another survivor, J. Elwood Sanders. "I saw about a dozen fellows going around helping themselves to the effects of the killed and wounded," he said. "I spoke to several thinking they were relatives or friends when they became embarrassed and walked away."

In the coroner's inquest, however, Pennington softened his stance, and survivor H. Harr Rowe told the jury that yes, valuables and personal effects were taken from the victims, but everything was returned to their families. Several others, including members of the families of the deceased, confirmed that no personal valuables were missing.

Wreck crews worked through the night to the light of giant bonfires which were built around the scene. Inside the rooms of the station, coal oil lamps and lanterns illuminated the grim work which continued into late Saturday night. It was said that the wooden floors of the station were soaked with blood, and the Lutz well was pumped dry twice during the emergency. "When the hotel floors were washed, " a reporter wrote, "buckets of water red with blood were swept out."

Most of the 29 people who died that night at Exeter Station never knew what hit them. Most died instantly as Engine 574 slammed into the Cannon Ball Express.

For the survivors, May 12, 1899 was a date they would never forget. George Lewis, who had been in a party mood as the special train rumbled from Reading toward his Norristown home, lamented to a reporter the day after the crash: "This is a sorry ending for a demonstration which we had all enjoyed so much. All the Norristown men who were in the party had fought with Hartranft's 51st Regiment, and had a most delightful day, meeting their old comrades again. I was riding on the third car from the rear of the special when the collision occurred. I was crushed by the shock and saw the passengers in the car thrown every way."

A simple testimonial to the force of the crash was the big, bass drum of the 51st Regiment Band. It was found several hours after the crash, in a field some 50 yards away from the railroad tracks.

132

The days between the collision and the funerals of Norristown's dead were gripping. Flags were flown at half-mast in the town, and most businesses were draped in black. Eventually, dry goods stores in Norristown exhausted their supplies of black cloth, and young men were sent into Philadelphia for more.

Two odd tales came out of Norristown in the wake of the wreck. Since Slingluff had also been president of the Prison Board, it was rumored that the board would issue a reprieve for a man who was slated to be hanged on May 18. No such request was, or could have been issued, as it turned out, since reprieves of persons on death row could only have come from the governor. The execution was carried out on schedule.

Survivors were said to have shown signs of insanity in the days following the wreck, and Harry Leister, of Phoenixville, one of those survivors, was interviewed two days after the crash and said he remembered nothing about any celebration in Harrisburg, any train wreck, or how he sustained his rather serious injuries.

And, before the grief caused by the wreck, many in Norristown were anxious to attend the Pawnee Bill Wild West Show, which was to be held there. Considering the pallor which had been cast over the town, the sponsors of the event attempted to cancel the show. After intense negotiations, and even the offer of several hundred dollars to "buy out" the appearance, Pawnee Bill refused to cancel his show. Popular opinion led to a virtual boycott of the show, and the borough refused to allow any street parade to herald it.

May 17 brought with it eight funerals in Norristown, including the final rites of Chief Slingluff. An estimated 5,000 people viewed his remains, and more than 1,000 men from fire companies, shrine units and other organiations in several states marched in the official funeral procession.

The railroad was a chief lifeline of

communications, cargo, and business in 1899. Thus, crews worked quickly and diligently to restore service as quickly as possible following the mishap, while Norristonians and all those affected by the collision worked to restore their lives.

After the wreckage was cleared and the damaged tracks were repaired, clean, white gravel was poured over the site. Still, the little village of Exeter was abuzz with those who came to see what they could see, and in some cases, take what they could take.

The lush embankment on the river side of the tracks was charred black as the ruined cars were burned, and small remnants of the shattering crash remained along the tracks for weeks after the wreck. Railroad workers had made every effort to pick up all items of personal property from the scene, but some gruesome discoveries were made by curious souvenir hunters in the days after the restoration of the rail service.

The Reading Eagle praised the response of the people of Exeter that fateful night:

"The usually quiet village is still visited by large numbers of persons from Reading, Birdsboro, and even more distant points. They saunter along the scorched side of the embankment, picking up fragments of iron, crumbled tin, charred wood or tattered remnantsof coats or other wearing apparel for relics.

"The spot where the crash took place is scarcely evident to the passengers who, on each passing train, still crowd to the windows to get a glimpse of the site.

"The patient people of Exeter Station and vicinity are tired of answering questions and explaining to visitors how things happened. Well-dressed ladies, with and without escorts, still arrive in fine turnouts, or by train, and start a conversation with anybody that happens along, expecting to hear something that has not been published in the papers."

The phrase, "Exeter Wreck," became so vexing to the residents of the little village and to railroad officials that the name of the station, and thus the village, was changed to Lorane shortly after the crash.

The train wreck of 1899 had forever altered the destiny of the village, the lives of hundreds of individuals, and the way the railroad went about its dispatching.

Twelve days after the accident, the Berks County Coroner's Jury reached a decision that Pennsylvania and Reading Trainmaster George Bowers in Philadelphia "used very bad judgement in equipping a special train with a crew unfamiliar with the main line division."

Bowers was held responsible for the incident, along with Dispatcher James J. Rourke, Engineer Daniel Wildermuth of the first section of Train No. 12, Engineer Harry Orrell of the second section and Conductor A.E. Mogue of the second second section. The latter four men were charged with "negligence, willful misconduct and failing to observe necessary precautions." and it was announced at the end of the coroner's inquest that the four men had already been arrested and held under $1,000 bail.

Berks County District Attorney Wilson H. Rothermel took charge of the investigation from that point, joining with the Berks County coroner, and Montgomery County coroner G.R. McGlathery in an even more intensive probe.

James Toal, an Exeter resident who said he witnessed the approach of the second section and the crash itself, told the jury he never saw the hind man of the first section run back, and never saw any danger signals displayed.

Jonas Schwartz, telegraph operator at Exeter, confirmed that after the coal train broke down at Birdsboro, he informed the dispatchers in Reading of the breakdown. William Fox, conductor of the coal train, confirmed that following orders from Reading, he shifted 50 of his 73 cars from the southbound to northbound track. He was well aware that the move blocked both tracks, but felt the matter would be resolved in the towers and telegraphs between there and Reading.

Throughout the hearings, dispatcher Rourke and Engineer Orrell levelled charges and counter-charges at one another. Rourke maintained that the necessary signals of danger were sent, but Orrell claimed he had seen no such warnings at any of the four towers between Reading and Exeter.

But, Thomas Geiger, who was stationed at one of the towers, asserted that he positively did display the red board. Furthermore, Calvin Lesher, operator at the Exeter Station, said he, too, put up the red signal, and produced the order handed down to him from Reading that night.

Interestingly, as the stories of the signal tower operators unfolded, it was discovered that one could not read, write or speak English, and another hadn't had his eyes examined for 11 years.

The tangled testimony continued, and the jury sorted through all details, eventually citing the individuals for their roles in the incident, but deciding to charge them with misdemeanors rather than criminal manslaughter. Still, the misdemeanor charge under the "Safety of Travelers on Railroads" act, carried a maximum punishment of five years in the state penitentiary and a five thousand dollar fine.

The jury also suggested that the railroad tighten its procedures. There had been in effect a rule which kept trains dispatched at no less than five-minute intervals. The investigators suggested that because of increased traffic, and particularly at night, the span between dispatched trains be expanded to at least ten minutes.

Further, the jury emphatically recommended that the entire signal system south of Reading be examined and revised. Orrell, who had appeared at the inquest wearing a bandage around his head, said the signalling system was antiquated, and while he as much as admitted to "reckless running," he said a telephone connection between the towers, and an automatic block system would probably have prevented the crash.

At Exeter, or Lorane, history had been made. The sleepy station had been the scene of bitter railroad strike activity in 1877, and a trainman was killed in a crash there in 1886, but nothing before orafter had so profoundly affected life in that corner of Berks County.

The station and hotel buildings still exist, but the sturdy brick structures are overgrown and forlorn. Across the tracks, nearly a century of growth has covered the embankment. No evidence remains of that ghastly night.

But as one stands beside the Conrail tracks and gazes toward the curve just north of the station, it is easy to stand in the shoes of Billy Lutz as he watched old Charlie Miller frantically wave his red lantern as Engine 574 barrelled around the bend.

The crackling, crunching sound of iron and wood will rumble in your imagination just as it echoed there so many years ago.

THE EXETER WRECK

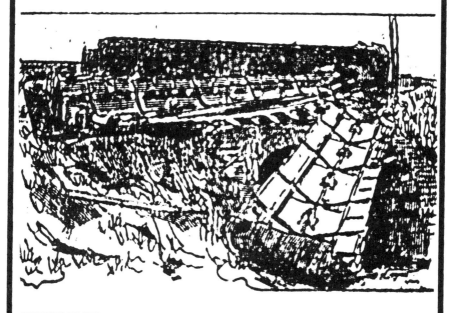

SKETCHES BY NEWSPAPER ARTISTS WERE DONE HASTILY UPON ARRIVAL AT THE SCENE OF THE WRECK. IN THE TOP VIEW, THE WRECKED PULLMAN CAR IS DEPICTED, WHILE IN THE LOWER SKETCH, A PASSENGER CAR IS SEEN SLICED IN TWO, WITH PART OF IT DOWN AN EMBANKMENT.

THE DEADLY PRANK
May 16, 1899
Tamaqua, Schuylkill County

For whatever reason, people seem to have a strange compulsion to place things on railroad tracks. Usually, it is nothing more than a penny, which, when a train rambles over it, squashes into an elongated slab of metal which serves as a strange trophy for the beholder.

While it is against all reason to put any item on any active railroad track, people do. Usually pennies.

The annals of railroad history are filled with stories of derailments and tragedies initiated by the careless, thoughtless, and sometimes deliberate placing of objects on railroad tracks.

At least one such act resulted in two deaths, and proved to be infinitely stupid and ultimately criminal.

Passenger train No. 4, consisting of a combination and a day coach, bound from Shamokin to Philadelphia on the Philadelphia and Reading line, was nearing the Zehner's flag station about four miles south of Tamaqua when it skipped from the southbound rails at Longacre's Curve.

As its engine teetered, a northbound freight was passing on the other track, and the passenger train locomotive sideswiped it, careened off about six freight cars, reared up, and flipped.

After the initial shock, all passengers were declared safe, but two crewmen were missing.

As wreck crews searched the twisted remains of

the engine and tender, they found engineer Samuel Grier's body crushed beneath the boiler. Nearby was fireman Lott Kerstetter, who was scalded to the point that he later died.

Railroad officials investigated, and found a partially-flattened railroad spike near the point where the passenger engine left the tracks.

After further checking, 17-year old Oliver Ohl, who lived nearby, was taken into custody as the train wrecker.

Ohl, who was working at a timber yard adjacent to the rail line, admitted that he put the spike on the tracks as a stunt, never intending to cause harm.

His co-workers agreed, but they said they warned him to remove the spike before a train came along and damage might be done. For reasons known only to himself, he did not remove the spike, and he paid the price.

Meanwhile, the two railroaders had paid a much more serious price for the wrecker's idea of a prank.

GREAT TRAIN WRECKS OF EASTERN
PENNSYLVANIA

PART TWO

THE
TWENTIETH
CENTURY

RETURN OF THE WRECKERS
November 23, 1903
Philadelphia

The 20th century would bring with it profound changes in the way railroads operated, and the way society coped with those changes.

The railroad companies, almost omnipotent in the last decades of the 19th century, would lose their bases of power, and as private automobiles, trucks, and then air traffic grew in volume, the influence and affluence of railroads shrank, almost in proportion.

The "romance" of the rails was over, the glitter of the "golden age" was fading, and in as many years as it took for Eastern Pennsylvania railroads to develop into powerful business giants, they fell into economic ruin.

The texture of the train wreck likewise changed as technology, regulation and public awareness caught up with what had been an almost untouchable mode of transportation.

Oil lanterns, signal boards and manual switches faded fast, and steam gave way to diesel. In 1945, there were more than 4,400 steam locomotives in service on American railroads. By 1950, that number was cut nearly in half. In 1957, the year many railroad historians consider to be the last year of the steam era, there were only about 450 steam engines on the lines.

In 1992, almost all of the steamers still active were on tourist excursion railroads.

As the power evolved, so did the equipment. Steel freight cars debuted on the Pennsylvania Railroad in 1898, but were not in common usage until 1913. By the

142

1940s, dangerous wooden cars were all but gone.

The Pennsy switched from 100 pound to 130 pound rail in 1920, and also upgraded its drainage, deepened its ballast and treated its ties. New signals were developed, new brakes, draft gear and couplers were developed, and employee training programs were improved.

The result was a steady decline in the railroad's casualty rate. In 1915, the Pennsylvania recorded 169 deaths and 4,255 injuries of passengers and employees. In 1925, 91 died and 2,208 were injured. From 1931 to 1936, the average yearly death toll was two, and an average of 344 persons were injured.

The Interstate Commerce Commission reported that in fiscal year 1899, the death rate on United States railroads was one passenger for every 2,200,000. Insurance companies responded to this safe manner of travel to the point that most included double indemnity clauses for policy holders injured or killed while riding in steam-powered conveyances.

Still, people found ways to die on the railroads. In the first decade of the 20th century, on the Pennsylvania Railroad alone, 8,523 people were killed as they trespassed on railroad property. That alarming figure prompted the railroad to post "no trespassing" signs, and increase its vigilance in its yards and along its rights-of-way.

As the 1900s progressed, however, so did corporate and private respect for the railroads and their properties. In 1976, the Federal Railroad Administration reported a total of 5,350 accidents on American freight and passenger railroads. Amtrak, which had then assumed the vast majority of American rail passenger service, experienced only 26 derailments that year, and only one other on the remaining inter-city railroad passenger lines which were not part of the Amtrak system.

Amtrak also boasted that in the first six years of its existence, only 12 passengers were killed on its lines.

Eleven of them died in one wreck in 1971 and the other perished in a 1973 accident. In the same time period, Amtrak officials pointed out, about 230,000 motorists lost their lives in highway accidents.

By 1984, Amtrak's safety record remained intact, with the F.R.A. reporting that the rail traffic safety record was indeed slightly better than air travel and 33 times better than on the highway.

The gist of all of this is that while you have read, and will continue to read sometimes sordid stories of railroad disasters, you may come away with the opinion that there has been a continual carnage on American rails. That is certainly not so. Should you add up all the fatalities in this volume, the number would probably not approach the total deaths in two major aircraft crashes.

The intent of this book is not to present graphic details of grisly death. It is, instead, to provide a chronological account of historically significant train wrecks in the heartland of American railroading.

As the stories shift into the second century of railroading in America, note the transitions not only in the type of railroad accidents but in the style of reporting which accompanied them. Not only did railroads face sweeping sociological, technological and economic changes, so did the nation's media.

In the 19th century, information was disseminated only by word-of-mouth and newspapers. With the advent of radio, and then television, sound and moving pictures created images in the public's mind which before could only be instilled by the printed word.

Thus, as we proceed to 1900, we shall witness a gradual shift in our focus.

In a 1901 paper, *Railway Wrecks and Wrecking,* by George Hebard Paine, the causes of railroad wrecks were placed into three categories: Mistakes in operation, defects of road and equipment, and miscellaneous.

Paine's first category included human error and disobedience, while the other two encompassed equipment

144

or road defects and failure.

Paine could not have known that by the midpoint of the 20th century, the leading cause of death on American railroads would be grade crossing accidents.

Certainly, train wrecks continued to claim lives and cause massive destruction and misery. But it is interesting that the first major train accident of the 1900s in Eastern Pennsylvania took place at a point where, quite simply, someone did not "stop, look and listen."

***

August 13, 1900
Near Slatington, Lehigh County

It was during a heavy thunderstorm on a lonely road just south of Slatington. A funeral procession of several omnibus coaches was traveling along a road when it approached the Lehigh & New England railroad crossing at what the locals called Benninger's Crossing.

Bill Benninger was at his farm when the horse-drawn coaches passed by. He wasn't paying particular attention, but testified later that he did notice that all proper signals were working as Train No. 6 on what was commonly called the "Poughkeepsie Route" was about to roll by.

Seconds before the signals heralded the oncoming westbound train, one of the omnibuses had safely crossed over the tracks. Another coach was close behind, with James Peters urging his steed through the S-curve along Lockport Creek.

Later, the driver of the first coach said he warned Peters not to attempt crossing in front of the train, but Peters took the chance.

Thirteen of the 28 passengers in the coach were killed.

In the coroner's inquest, Peters, and the crew of the train were blamed for the collision, and Benninger said he detected the odor of whiskey on Peter's breath when he pulled him out of the wreckage.

145

Three days later, in Hereford, Berks County, another grade crossing accident resulted in the deaths of three persons, and the new perils of the 20th century, as increased railroad traffic and increased vehicular traffic clashed, intensified.

"A FIEND INCARNATE"
November 21, 1903
Philadelphia

By mere feet, a catastrophe was averted on the Bethlehem Division of the Philadelphia and Reading Railroad that Saturday night in November.

However, it was felt by some observers that an even more destructive wreck was prevented by a broad stroke of fate.

The Doylestown local of two passenger and one combination car left Doylestown at 10:25 p.m., and was due at Reading Terminal just before midnight. Several passengers, fresh from a wedding anniversary party in Lansdale, clustered in the front car.

The train dropped off a passenger at the Gwynedd station, and maintained a slow speed a few hundred more yards toward the stone arch bridge which carried it some 40 feet over the Wissahickon Creek.

Edward McCourt was engineer on the run, but he was allowing Harry Roderick, his fireman, to get some practice at the throttle, while McCourt did the firing.

As the train chugged slowly onto the bridge, Roderick and McCourt knew something was going wrong. The engine wobbled, bumped and thumped, and it was obvious it had left the rails. Miraculously, the locomotive hobbled on the ties, precariously lurching its way across the bridge. At the southern end, when solid ground was reached, the engine became hopelessly unstable, and slid from the rail bed. The first coach followed suit.

They rolled down a relatively gently-sloping

147

embankment, and the first and second cars remained coupled. The second and third cars did not derail, and their weight held the first coach back from an even more disastrous fall down the hill. Several large trees also blocked the train from further damage.

The only passenger casualty was Clement Custer, a member of the wedding anniversary party who was thrown through a window of the coach as it teetered off the tracks. That coach then rolled over on top of the victim.

McCourt and Roderick went down with their engine. Both were in the cab as it fell down the embankment. McCourt survived, scalded and bruised, but the 39-year old Roderick was not as lucky. While he survived the roll of the engine, he was tossed from the cab at the bottom of the hill, and the water tank of the tender spilled onto him, drowning him.

McCourt's injuries were intense, but he managed to scramble back to the tracks and direct the rescue operations.

He had been there before.

Eight years before, he was forced to break through the window of his cab with his bare hands while trapped in an avalanche during a blizzard in a cut along the West Jersey line. Earlier, as a fireman, he escaped injury in a collision on the P & R. He went to work the next day, but was sent home because the railroad had already taken on a substitute for him, figuring he would not report so soon after the harrowing escape. Two hours later, his replacement that day was killed in another wreck!

"The pluckiest thing I ever saw," said crash witness H.H. Nusson, "was that engineer, with his face and hands horribly scalded, walking around there and directing the others how to rescue the imprisoned passengers in the cars. He told us to break the windows and drag the men and women out."

It was obvious from the very start of the investigation that someone had deliberately caused the

148

wreck. What's more, there was speculation that the wrecker, described by Charles A. Beach, superintendent of the Bethlehem Division, as a "fiend incarnate," may have targeted another train.

The Black Diamond Express, which was known to carry cars laden with veritable fortunes in money, may have been the true target of the wrecker.

The Black Diamond was a connecting train, and while it was due at that bridge at around 10 p.m. that night, it was often late. The night of the wrecker's deed, however, it passed right on time.

That the express carried vast sums consigned to express agencies had some believe it was the wrecker's intent to derail the train and rob it during the chaos.

It was more than theory that the wreck was caused by someone with some knowledge of the railroad system. The fishplates and angle irons were yanked out, thus separating the rail. And, nine spikes were removed, the rail was pulled back about six inches and spiked to the ties. But, the villain knew enough not to cut into the bond wires of the block signal system. Had they done that, a red light would have shown on the signal post, alerting the engineer to the trouble.

Knowing that, wrecking crewmen sought the tools which would have been used to separate the rails. Sure enough, after sloshing in the shallow water of the Wissahickon, they retrieved a crowbar and wrench, each with the railroad's logo emblazoned on them. The tools had recently been stolen from a tool shed at the North Wales tunnel.

Suspicion centered on what investigators called "a band of Negroes" who lived in the area Lansdale. William Steever, the engine wiper, told detectives, "They have been regular passengers on the train leaving the Reading Terminal every Saturday night. Every time they get on the train they cause trouble."

Steever continued, "The colored men have been in an ugly mood for some time past, and I think they have been trying to get square with the train crew."

A friend of Roderick, the fireman who died in the wreck, said he wanted to take a blackjack and pistol with him to work that night, fully expecting further trouble from the "colored men."

Roderick's sister later said he had not taken the weapons with him. "He anticipated trouble simply because it was Saturday night and after payday, when workmen are likely to get drunk."

The railroad brought in Pinkerton agents in addition to its own detective force, and the entire division was scoured, and virtually everyone who worked on it or lived along it was questioned. Even two bloodhounds were brought down from Elmira, N.Y., by William Cloudman. But Billy and Eddy had no more luck than the Pinkertons in finding the suspect.

THEY WERE BLOWN TO ATOMS
May 11, 1905
Harrisburg

The job of a good reporter is to get the news out fast and factually. In haste, and perhaps with all good intentions, this job is often only half accomplished.

There is no doubt that when folks picked up their morning newspapers that Thursday morning they were startled to read of what could easily have been the most horrible train wreck in history.

The Eastern Express had collided with another train in South Harrisburg, and an estimated 163 people were dead. Many of the victims were, as the initial accounts read, "blown to atoms," and "no trace of them will ever be found."

The train was the Cleveland and Cincinnati Express, and as it turned out, thankfully, the final death count was 22. The cause of the wreck was, frightfully, obvious.

The express pulled out of Philadelphia at 11:05 the previous night, and aboard it were several notables of the day. The daughter of a U.S. Senator, the wife of the Pittsburgh Post publisher, the son-in-law of the assistant to the president of the Pennsylvania Railroad, and the legendary Sam S. Shubert, the New York theatrical magnate.

The trip from Philadelphia to Harrisburg was uneventful, but when the express reached the south Harrisburg yards, something terrible happened.

A switcher was maneuvering through the yards as

an eastbound freight train bore down on it. The engineer of the 68-car freighter pulled the air brakes and his train screeched to a halt. As the result of the action, however, a boxcar 34 cars in back of the engine buckled in the middle and leaned into the westbound tracks.

Its timing, and its cargo, could not have been worse. The express was steaming at breakneck speed, directly into the path of the listing boxcar. The freight train crew had no time to send up a danger signal, it was far too late to stop the passenger train, and its engineer, H.K. Thomas, somehow felt it could clear the boxcar.

It could not.

The boxcar was filled with dynamite.

The Pullman car "Socrates" sideswiped the boxcar, and in a flash, a chain reaction of explosions rocked both trains, blowing the passenger locomotive to smithereens and touching off a monumental fire.

Like blazing dominoes, the freight and passenger cars were swept by flames. Gas tanks popped, shot through the roofs of the coaches, and the inferno consumed car after car, person after person.

Many of the passengers had been asleep, and were hard pressed to face the cold, dark night. Still, some nearly naked, those who survived the initial blast scrambled across cinders and ballast to flee the fire. Some of the passengers were catapulted out of the exploding cars and into the Susquehanna River. Some never made it out of their coaches.

There was no need to summon emergency help. Windows were blown out of houses a mile away, and fire fighters easily pinpointed the source of the explosion.

Neighbors responded with supplies and manpower to help in the rescue, but the damage was inconceivable.

Ten charred and unrecognizable bodies were found in the Pullman, and Engineer Thomas' mutilated body was found on the bank of the river. He had been blown through the roof of the cab when the boiler

152

exploded.

Sam Shubert survived the initial explosions and fire, and was pulled out of the wreckage by Abe Thalheimer, one of his traveling companions.

"I was not scalded or burned," Thalheimer said after the accident, "and I crawled out of the window with nothing on but my pajamas. I made my way down the embankment at the side of the railroad, and then I thought of Sam.

"By the light of the burning cars I could see him pinned in his berth. Crawling up on a portion of the car which had been blown off, I managed to get at Mr. Shubert, and tried to arouse him to a sense of his danger. 'Go away a let me die,' he pleaded, but I simply answered, 'not today,' and pulled him back from the car.

"In my bare feet I climbed down over the sharp stones of the embankment, again carrying Sam on my back. I put him down on the river bank and then got a car cushion for him to rest on, and grabbed a carpet from the floor to cover him."

Despite his friend's heroics, Sam Shubert lost his battle for life in the hospital the day after the accident.

By the middle of the night, about 1,000 railroad crewmen were on the scene, laboring to clear the tracks and restore service to the line.

As it turned out, many of the wild reports from the scene at the outset proved to be grossly exaggerated. The initial estimate of 163 deaths was far higher than the final casualty total of 23. It was discovered that none of the gas tanks beneath the coaches actually exploded, and the locomotives involved were not damaged beyond repair.

What was looked upon at first as a wreck which would cost the railroad at least a million dollars in damages wound up costing about one-third that sum. Of course, that total was based on the fact that the average accident claim settled upon with the passengers was $250.

Three passengers were apparently "blown to atoms," as the reporter so graphically put it in the first story filed from the scene. Their bodies were never recovered, but personal effects and testimony from other passengers verified that they had been on the train before the explosion. Even though the bodies were not found, the railroad settled with their families, and included their names on a monument in the Paxtang Cemetery, where other unidentified remains were buried at the railroad's expense.

As for the explosion itself, the bill of lading showed that the boxcar which was struck was filled with ten tons of Judson Rock Chief Powder, a blasting powder consisting of seven percent dynamite. The powder was destined for the H.S. Kerbaugh Co. of Columbia, Pa.

The cause of the accident was determined to be related to the fact that some cars on the freight trains had air brakes and others had hand brakes. That mixture, experts said, could be dangerous in emergencies.

The Pennsylvania Railroad was not held to blame for the accident, and all crews of the shifting engine, the freight and the express were exonerated.

The accident in Harrisburg that day spurred legislators to re-examine the way explosives were carried on American railroads. Railroaders testified at the coroner's inquest that shippers sometimes concealed dangerous cargoes with innocuous labels.

Passenger cars and freight cars carrying dynamite were sometimes coupled together, and it was not unusual for explosives to be loosely packed in freight cars.

Two days after the Harrisburg wreck, a bill was introduced in the U.S. Senate which put more strict regulations on the shipping, labeling, inspection and packing of explosives on American railroads.

***

January 16, 1907
Bridgeport, Mongtomery County

A low water level in the boiler of an Allentown-to-Philadelphia freight engine was blamed for the deaths of five railroad crewmen in an explosion in Bridgeport.

The wheels of the engine stayed on the tracks, but the back of the boiler was tossed 150 feet by the blast. Only the engineer survived the accident.

***

July 2, 1907
Sunbury, Northumberland County

The Buffalo Express and a freight train collided on the Pennsylvania Railroad when the engineer of the passenger train did not see the freight backing off the main tracks.

Three persons on the express were killed, and the baggage and express cars of the passenger train were reduced to rubble.

***

October 14, 1907
Pottstown, Montgomery County

Four persons, including a one-year old child, were killed when the car in which they were riding was struck by a Reading Railroad express at the Keim Street crossing.

***

August 1, 1908
Philadelphia

Two men, trying to beat a train to the Hunting Park grade crossing, lost the race and their lives as their "machine" was struck broadsides by the train. The driver had ignored the safety gates, which were down.

***

July 4, 1913
Shelly, Bucks County

Independence Day proved fatal for five persons

whose picnic wagon was hit by the Scranton Flyer on the North Penn Branch of the Philadelphia and Reading Railroad. The party of eight in the wagon was returning from a Fourth of July celebration in Hellertown. Andrew Glass, engineer of the train, said, "The picnic wagon was racing to beat out the train. I saw it directly ahead. Quick as a flash I threw on the brakes, but it was too late. It was impossible to stop in such a short distance. The sight that met my eyes when I did stop was the most awful I ever saw. Fragments of the bodies were scattered along the roadway, and the injured lay in a mangled heap under the wagon." The train engine almost derailed when the carcasses of the dead horses were wedged firmly under the cowcatcher.

As the 20th Century was unfolding, railroading was undergoing profound changes. Indeed, the *world* was changing.

Drivers of "machines," or automobiles, were taunting trains at crossings, horses were enjoying their last gasps as the favored form of transportation, and history was being made as the fruits of the industrial revolution were ripening.

The day of the Pottstown train-auto crash, Guglielmo Marconi announced that commercial wireless telegraph service between Britain and the United States may be ready for service by the end of October, 1907.

On January 28, 1911, when two persons died when an express train and a freight collided near Chalfont, the Hope Diamond, which had been cut to 44.5 carats, was sold to a New Yorker for $300,000, despite superstitions that it was cursed.

And on June 29, 1911, as one passenger died and more than a score were injured in the underground tunnel near the Reading Terminal, the White Star line announced forthcoming deployment plans which would be necessary when its new ship, the Titanic, was put into service in ten months. The ship deployments were to be coordinated to avoid competition with the Cunard Line's pride, the

Lusitania.

On the rails that day, the Chestnut Hill Express was entering the tunnel at 21st and Hamilton Streets when engineer Ben Dolan ignored warning signals and sideswiped a freight train. One man, who was sitting in the first seat of the car directly in back of the engine, was killed when the side of the car caved in on him.

* * *

February 11, 1912
Conestoga Junction, Lancaster County

More than fifty members of the Chicago-Philadelphia Grand Opera Company were shaken up when the piston rod of their train broke.

* * *

July 27, 1913
Slatington, Lehigh County

One person was killed and more than two dozen were injured when two freight trains collided and an express passenger train slammed into their wreckage.

Investigators credited air brakes and steel cars for averting, "what could have been recorded as one of the worst horrors in the history of railroad disasters."

* * *

July 5, 1915
Hummelstown, Dauphin County

A wagon pulled by two mules and carrying six people who were returning home from a Fourth of July celebration in Hummelstown was struck by a P & R train as the wagon attempted to cross the tracks ahead of the express.

* * *

February 26, 1917
Bristol, Bucks County

Little Jewel, Bell Cord, Al Direct and fourteen others were killed in the most disastrous train wreck ever in Eastern Pennsylvania, for horses.

The steeds were on a train which was also loaded with more than 30 cars of perishable food bound for New York.

The axle on a car in a westbound freight snapped, and the car toppled onto the adjoining tracks. The Adams Express special train, carrying the food, newsprint, horses, horsemen and its crew, steamed along, struck the downed car, and was wrecked.

Four men were killed in addition to the show horses, and neighbors are said to have had a field day rummaging through the wreck for fresh food for their pantries.

* * *

March 15, 1918
Elizabethtown, Lancaster County

As World War I raged on overseas, two persons died and more than two dozen when hundreds of tons of earth fell upon the Cincinnati, Indianapolis and Chicago Express as it rambled through the Elizabethtown cut between Harrisburg and Lancaster.

Several soldiers, who were in an undamaged smoking car, helped in the rescue efforts.

* * *

January 13, 1919
Fort Washington, Montgomery County

The Doylestown Local, filled with men and women who had completed their day's labors at the Midvale Steel plant and other factories along the line, was coming into the Fort Washington station when its engineer noticed a derailed locomotive on the tracks ahead, and halted his train.

Within minutes, the Scranton Flier zoomed around the curve which leads into the station and slammed into the local.

The last car of the local, described as an "old wooden type," was crushed, and nine passengers were killed.

IRON HORSE vs HORSEPOWER

AS MOTORISTS TOOK TO THE OPEN ROAD, BOTH THEY AND THE RAILROADS FACED NEW HAZARDS, AS SEEN IN THIS PHOTO FROM THE READING *EAGLE*.

"COFFIN CARS" IN "DEATH GULCH"

December 5, 1921
Bryn Athyn, Montgomery County

The world news headline of the day informed readers that after the uprising on the Emerald Isle, Ireland appeared to have won partial independence from Britain. Ulster (Northern Ireland) would remain under British control while the rest of the country would gain its sovereignty.

But in Philadelphia, the big story was a big train wreck, two miles north of Bryn Athyn, on the Newtown Division of the Philadelphia and Reading Railroad.

It was not a pretty sight. It was a wreck of 19th century proportions, made even more devastating because the cars involved were of 19th century vintage.

After the accident, locals took to calling the deep cut in which 23 people were killed "death gulch," or the "valley of death." They took to calling the antiquated wooden cars which contributed to their deaths "coffin cars."

The commuters on the busy suburban line, and others like it in the Reading system, were obliged to continue to ride in the wooden vestibuled coaches, since they were virtually all the Reading used on those runs. But following the Bryn Athyn tragedy, few folks settled for seats near the front of the train.

The timing, the place and the circumstances surrounding the wreck were all wrong. They were the ingredients for catastrophe, and at a little past eight

161

o'clock that Monday morning, catastrophe it was.

Charles Evans was right on time. His three-car up-train had pulled out of the Reading Terminal at 6:48. Charley was the conductor of that train, No. 151, and Walter Yeakel was engineer.

When they reached Bryn Athyn, station agent Russel Clayton gave Evans his orders: "Train No. 151 will meet No. 156 at Bryn Athyn. No. 151 take siding." Evans read and signed for them. He instructed the crew to hold at Bryn Athyn until No. 156 passed by.

As Yeakel and Evans waited at the loop for about ten minutes, a southbound local roared through.

There was nothing terribly out of the ordinary about this passing. However, the local and the up-train usually crossed south of Bryn Athyn. That morning, the local was running late, and for whatever reason, Yeakel and Evans apparently thought the local was the No. 156 down train. After the local went by, they started back toward Newtown.

Clayton was in the station talking with fellow workers when he saw the 151 pull out. He knew it was running against orders, and wondered what was going on. Frantically, he ran after the up train, shouting and waving wildly to the brakeman. The train continued along.

They made it only as far as "death gulch."

In 1876, the deep cut was one of several made into rocky hills for the former Philadelphia and Newtown Railroad. It was in a remote, wooded section along the Pennypack Creek.

Russel Clayton knew as soon as the 151 returned to the track that disaster was imminent. He knew the 156 was coming down, and he knew that the double tracks narrowed to one at the cut. He knew there would be a major head-on collision.

His diligence may have averted even more deaths. As the 151 steamed out of sight, Clayton ran back to the Bryn Athyn station and placed a call to the Abington Hospital, the Reading Railroad office, and to his brother,

William, the station master at Woodmont, on the other end of the cut. As he alerted all to the impending crash, the sound of the two engines meeting in the cut rattled from beyond. Russel Clayton's worst fears had been realized.

As the up train built speed out of Bryn Athyn, Train No. 156 was roaring south. Its five coaches were filled with passengers who boarded at Newtown, and were headed for Philadelphia. The train,which was to arrive at the terminal at 8:30 a.m., was among the most popular in the entire suburban system.

James Rook was at the throttle of the 156, and acting on orders, he delayed his train at Woodmont, where he expected the northbound 151 to pass on the double tracks. New signals were displayed, and Rook was instructed to proceed south.

He brought the train no farther than a quarter-mile southeast of Woodmont when he entered the cut. Its rocky walls were more than 30 feet high, and railroad men called it "the tunnel without a roof."

The tracks at that point narrowed to one set, and the doomed trains were on a collision course of mammoth proportions.

Both trains were running at high speeds, neither engineer had any idea the other was approaching, and with a force that literally shook the earth there, the 151 and the 156 slammed together in the rocky cut.

There were only about five feet of space on either side of the chasm, and there was no room for the engines to go but up. When they met with such overpowering force, they shoved one another up, wrenched and twisted and were joined by the tenders, and with an enervating roar, smacked onto the rail bed as one mass of broken metal.

Fire broke out immediately. The wooden coaches, by then piled onto the smoldering fireboxes, became nothing more than kindling for a blaze which would incinerate countless passengers in a matter of minutes.

"Countless" is an accurate word, since several individuals' bodies were never found, but piles of ashes around shards of human bones indicated their presence, and the intensity of the fire.

There was no escape from the pyre. Like a boiling cauldron, the flames and smoke spread in the tight confines of the cut, consuming all in their paths.

Forrest Edelman was one who survived the collision. He was on his way to work in Philadelphia, and was seated in the rear car of the down train. After the crash, which only jolted his car, he ventured front to see what had happened.

> *When we got up front, and saw the piled up*
> *wreckage, and the fire spreading, I knew that*
> *many persons were dead, or doomed to die,*
> *in that hell of fire, boiling hissing steam, and*
> *twisted metal. We got several out, and were*
> *driven back from the cars by the fire. On the*
> *bank, I saw the body of one dead man. Before*
> *I left the scene of the wreck, I saw at least four*
> *persons dead in that first coach, pinioned to*
> *their seats, or burned to a crisp.*

Rescue and medical crews were already on their way to the scene, thanks to the Clayton brothers. Even with this quick response, it was too late. The screams, moans and groans of the dying rose above the roar of the fire.

One man pleaded with a rescuer to bash in his skull lest he be consumed by fire. Another was burned to death as volunteers watched from the high top of the ravine, unable to reach him.

Piles of bones and ashes were carried out in potato baskets. The charred corpse of a baby was removed by an emotionally-drained fireman.

Those fire fighters struggled to secure water from the creek and wedge their way into the narrow cut to reach the victims and quell the flames. Mud and snow on the ground all around only complicated matters.

As the rescue efforts continued, railroad and government officials arrived to assess the damage and probe the cause. They wasted no time in offering preliminary decisions.

Vice president Ewing of the railroad said it appeared that Train No. 151 simply overran its orders. Mongtomery County Coroner William Neville agreed, and further commented that the wooden coaches were contributing factors to the high death toll.

That count was to reach 26, after all remains were accounted for in the morgues and mortuaries to which the ashes and bodies were taken.

Could many of these people have been spared if steel coaches were in service on that line, at that time? Could the entire tragedy been averted if orders had been followed?

Those questions were paramount in the minds of investigators from the railroad, the Pennsylvania Public Service Commission, the Interstate Commerce Commission, the agencies which held the inquiry.

Coroner Neville was left out of the investigation, but he was not shy when asked to comment on the matter. "Wooden coaches were responsible for the huge loss of life," he said. But what's the use of talking about wooden coaches? The railroad has these coaches, is using them, and when there is a wreck of this sort a heavy toll of life is exacted."

Some people criticized the use of a single track on such a busy line. It was estimated that the final cost of all damages and claims as the result of the Bryn Athyn Wreck would exceed a million dollars. The estimated cost of building a double-track line on the Newton Division was far below that figure.

These factors aside, the investigative team was interested most in fixing the blame for the crash. From the start of the probe, that blame seemed to be placed squarely on the shoulder of one man.

165

He was the man who received clearly-written orders, on standard-size writing paper, to keep his train in the Bryn Athyn siding until the local, Train No. 154, and then the down train, No. 156, passed by. He was the man who, authorities said, either disobeyed or bungled the orders and took his train north, and in the path of the 156 and "death gulch."

He was the conductor of the up train, Charles T. Evans.

While Evans later denied it, a witness testified he saw the battered conductor walking around the wreck scene, crying "Oh, my God, they will blame me for this, and I will be sent to prison!"

Evans, who had been working on the railroad for 22 years, was in complete charge of the up train that morning.

Railroaders said there was no excuse for Evans, or anyone else on the crew of his train, to mistake the local for the down train.

Furthermore, Bryn Athyn station master Clayton said he definitely gave Evans the instructions, and Evans definitely signed for them. "I didn't come here to convict Charley Evans," Clayton testified. "We are brother workers on the railroad and I want to say that a report that I blamed Evans for the wreck is not true. I did receive the order over the wire and gave Evans two copies of it, for which he signed. Then as the train pulled out I ran after it. That is all to my part of the wreck."

Investigators concluded that it was not all to Evans' part in the wreck, however.

As the conductor awaited his fate at the hands of the inquiry board, his wife at home in Norristown took ill, succumbing to the pressure which surrounded the case.

The investigation was thorough, and damning not only toward one worker, but an entire railroad line.

The signal system, or lack of it, on the Newtown Division was described as a holdover from the last century. Indeed, a 5.5 mile distance between Bryn Athyn and Churchville, which included "death gulch" and the single track strip, had no signal towers whatsoever.

The Huntingdon Valley block signal, the last such automatic signal north, was out of order on the fatal Monday morning.

And, the up train could not have pulled out of the Bryn Athyn siding had not a crewman opened a manual switch to allow it to re-enter the track. That crewman should have been stopped from doing so if the conductor of the train had paid attention and followed orders.

The blame seemed to center even more on Evans, and perhaps others in his crew.

On February 18, 1922, Evans and engineer Walter Yeakel were found guilty of negligence for their parts in the events which led to the collision. Two days later, they were sentenced to jail for six to nine months, and fined $500 each. The jury had recommended mercy, and they received it.

In May, Pennsylvania's governor pardoned both men, based on petitions to the state pardon board.

The pitiful signaling system on the line was cited by the investigators, but the railroad was not held responsible for the wreck. No laws or regulations had been violated.

But something was becoming quite clear as witness after witness decried the continued use of wooden coaches in the age of steel.

The Reading hadn't purchased steel cars since the turn of the century. Those used the morning of the collision were deemed in good shape, and had been in use for twenty years.

Still, the railroad was feeling pangs of guilt. It intimated that it may begin to replace all wooden cars with steel ones.

As Coroner Neville, still miffed that he was not included in the inquiry, continued to assail the railroad for the use of the wooden cars, Pennsylvania Lt. Gov. Edward Beidleman asserted that there should be legislation prohibiting the use of what he called "antique" wooden passenger cars in the state.

"It has been many years since I rode in one of these obsolete wooden coaches," Beidleman said. "I had thought they were entirely out of use until I read of this wreck. The wooden cars, which used to wobble from side to side, are a danger in themselves. The safety of the people should be carefully guarded," he concluded.

The families of the 26 people who died that December morning likely read the statement and tossed it aside. This hindsight was far too late for them and their loved ones who never made it home from "Death Gulch."

THE STEEL SAVIOR
September 27, 1928
Bethlehem, Northampton County

Through the 1920s, the same basic causes led to railroad accidents.

Engineer William Graham died, but no passengers were seriously injured when a 12-car Lehigh Valley mixed train derailed on Hell Gate Mountain, north of Wilkes-Barre on February 17, 1926. A broken brake beam caused the engine and half of its cars to leave the tracks. Equipment failure.

Another Lehigh Valley express slammed into a standing train after the express ran a block signal near Rummerfield, south of Towanda on February 20, 1928. Six crewmen were killed. Human error.

And, a bizarre wreck took place on July 24, 1928 in Philadelphia. Seventy fully-laden freight cars started to move at the top of a two-mile grade, and as they reached the bottom, crashed into a Pennsylvania Railroad engine, which in turn crashed into five other engines in the yards. There were no injuries. Gravity.

As the cities and towns of Eastern Pennsylvania grew both in area and population, the public's relationship with railroad rights-of-way grew more precarious.

January 12, 1933; Easton: Lehigh Valley engineer Clyde Hineline's body is found alongside the tracks, struck by a train.

169

February 18, 1933; Philadelphia: Real estate agent Folger Barker was struck and killed by a train in Roxborough.

December 21, 1933; Philadelphia: Fred Friend, one of several men who ventured onto railroad tracks to gather coals for their home furnaces, was hit by a Pennsy express train. He died on the spot.

September 20, 1926; Stowe, Montgomery County: Four section gang workers were killed when an express train barreled through their work site. The workers were using a tamping machine propelled by a gasoline engine as they worked on the tracks, and the sound of the engine drowned out the whistle of the approaching train.

Trespassing, ignorance and derring-do continued to claim lives by the hundreds. And, of course, the clash between trains, cars and trucks intensified as vehicular traffic increased.

September 2, 1928; Stroudsburg: A milk train smashed into a car carrying four passengers, killing all. The watchman at the Gravel Place crossing said he tried to warn the driver of the oncoming train, but he ignored him.

October 21, 1928; Wilkes-Barre: Several cars scrambled to beat the crossing gates, preventing the watchman from lowering them before a Jersey Central express breezed through the Scott Street crossing. Several autos were struck by the train, and three people were killed.

February 15, 1932; Philadelphia: A truck carrying six stevedores to the Delaware River piers, was struck by a freight train after the driver of the truck tempted fate at a grade crossing. He and four others were killed outright.

"I'm all in. I'm gone. It's all over." Those were the last words of E. F. Kilroy, engineer of the Seaboard Air Line express after his train overran a switch at Marcus Hook, Delaware County, on February 27, 1928.

His engine and five cars vaulted across three sets of tracks before coming to rest, its boiler blown out.

170

The P.R.R. express was running exceedingly late and, investigators thought, exceedingly fast through the switches. None of the passengers on board was injured. Investigators said there might have been many casualties if the cars were not made of steel.

Previous incriminations regarding wooden coaches were still fresh on the public's mind in the 1920s and 1930s. Some of the older, wooden coaches were still in use, but a rising sentiment demanded the safer (and costlier) steel cars be put into service.

The gradual implementation of steel cars was not an instant panacea. Cars still telescoped, cars still rolled down embankments, and cars still caught fire. But as the second and third generations of steel passenger cars came on the line, reinforced and improved, rail travel became infinitely safer.

To that end, what could have been an absolute disaster in Bethlehem on September 27, 1928 was averted, and steel coach No. 898 was given most of the credit.

Still, eight people died and three dozen were injured in a wreck on the Lehigh Division of the sometimes star-crossed Lehigh Valley Railroad.

The time: Sunrise. The place: At the new Union Station, at the foot of the new Hill-to-Hill Bridge, Bethlehem.

The Scranton Flyer, passing through the Christmas City on its way from Syracuse, N.Y., to Philadelphia, on the Central Railroad of New Jersey tracks, crashed into the Lehigh Limited at the crossroads of the two roads.

The 11-car Limited, a L.V.R.R. showpiece, was slowing into the station when the Flier ran through signals that several witnesses later affirmed those signals were warning it to stop for the Limited.

The second coach was struck broadside by the Jersey Central engine. The engine then slammed into a bridge abutment while the Pullman was pushed into a steel bridge girder and a Union Station platform.

171

Within minutes, the Hill-to-Hill Bridge was overcrowded with spectators. William Halteman, Bethlehem police chief, was quick on the scene, and soon dozens of officers and emergency workers pitched in to aid in the rescue efforts and clear the way for ambulances.

Northampton County Coroner Walter Cathrall assembled a coroner's jury on the scene, and the investigation was begun immediately.

The trains were supposed to be separated by ten minutes at the crossing. It was clearly established in the inquiry that the Jersey Central train was ahead of its appointed time, and overran the signals.

Henry Schmidt, a 19-year railroading veteran, was at the throttle of the Flyer, and hit his brakes when he saw the Limited looming at the crossing. Henry Conlin, engineer of the Limited, had already applied his brakes as he approached the station. Schmidt, of Mauch Chunk, later asserted that had the Limited been moving faster, the accident might not have happened. Schmidt and Conlin were later arrested on misdemeanor charges of disregarding signals.

* * *

January 30, 1936
Sunbury, Northumberland County

The Williamsporter, one of the most prestigious passenger express trains on the Reading Railroad, was about to cross the bridge from West Sunbury to East Sunbury when, for some reason unknown at the time, it careened off the tracks, into a bridge support, and into the old bed of the Pennsylvania Canal adjacent to the river.

Two sleeper cars and a coach followed the engine over a 25-foot embankment into the canal bed, and the engine continued to roll into the Susquehanna River.

As the train struck the bridge piling, a portion of the span collapsed, and telephone and telegraph wires were snapped.

Debris from the wreck fell onto a state highway

172

below, and created another hazard. The first ambulance to attempt to reach the scene crashed into the debris, and rescue workers could get no closer than a quarter-mile by car. They were forced to walk that distance to the wreck in a driving snowstorm and 15-degree temperatures.

When emergency crews finally reached the wreck, three bodies were pulled out, and more than 30 people were hurried to a Sunbury hospital with injuries.

It was discovered later that the express had rolled over a broken rail while it was rounding a curve approaching the bridge.

That winter had been particularly cold, and the Reading was shipping anthracite coal at a pace not experienced since World War I. The accident on that stretch of rail proved to be especially vexing for the railroad, and within hours of the wreck, the Reading struck a deal with the Pennsylvania Railroad to use the Pennsy's tracks between Shamokin and Sunbury for its busy coal trains until the rails and the bridge at Sunbury could be repaired.

* * *

October 24, 1937
Portland, Northampton County

There were some anxious moments for members of the Duke University football team when the train on which they were riding crashed into a Lackawanna Railroad milk train.

The gridders were returning from their game at Colgate, when the accident took place on a portion of the Pennsylvania line which was undergoing construction at the time. Three train crewmen were injured, but the Blue Devils were only shaken from their sleep.

* * *

October 31, 1940
Philadelphia

Graphic proof that the transportation system of the region had begun to evolve came in what was one of the first, and most frightening wrecks which brought steam and electric motive power together in a wreck which sounded and looked more devastating than it really turned out to be.

The sun was setting that Halloween night, and hundreds of commuters were at Logan Station in center-city Philadelphia, awaiting the trains which would take them home.

Confusion seemed to reign that evening at the busy station off Broad Street. A Baltimore & Ohio passenger train was proceeding on the Reading line at the Newtown Junction, and the Bethlehem Express was waiting for it to pass.

The four-car express was about to pull out when a two-car electric commuter train bound for Jenkintown struck the rear of the larger steamer.

Shocked passengers, pedestrians, motorists and onlookers watched as the trains collided with a deafening roar.

Philadelphia police patrolman William Clark was there.

"I heard what sounded like a whale of an explosion," he said. "I looked up. There was a flash of light, and the whole bridge was trembling."

To make matters worse, the electric current carrier, the pantograph, atop the commuter, was broken from its mounting on impact, and fell onto another track. Sure enough, an express train came along on that track within moments, but only shoved the pantograph aside as it passed.

While the front car of the commuter had telescoped into the rear car of the express, there was no fire and the 100 persons injured sustained relatively minor injuries.

The engineman of the electric train was later blamed by the railroad for operating his train too fast for conditions.

THE WRECK OF THE "CONGRESSIONAL LIMITED"
Labor Day, September 6, 1943
Philadelphia

The nation was at war. The nation's railroads played a major role on the home front, shuttling supplies, personnel and equipment at a pace and proportions unequaled in history.

With this incredible burden placed on trains during the war years, the risk factor was sure to rise. After all, steam was enjoying its last gasp, manpower shortages at home translated to short-cuts in maintenance of roads and rolling stock, and most lines simply didn't have the time or people to dedicate to safety.

In the first half of 1943, there were more than 8,200 rail accidents reported in the United States, the most ever in a six-month period.

The majority of those accidents were operational, and passenger and crew fatalities were, thankfully, at a minimum. But on Labor Day, in the Frankford section of Philadelphia, calamity was to strike in a merciless wreck of one of the pride and joys of the Pennsylvania Railroad, the Congressional Limited.

The Limited passed through Philadelphia on its 13-hour run from Washington to New York. It was one of the most prestigious express trains of its day, and on that beautiful fall holiday, it was filled with passengers, including hundreds of military men and women.

As the crack express sped around a curve at

176

Frankford, the engineer of a switcher engine noticed something untoward. Smoke, and then flames, shot from a journal box on the seventh car of the Limited. He knew it was overheating, and he knew the consequences could be dire.

The engineer shouted to a yard worker, who in turn telephoned a signal tower up the line, advising the signalman of the "hotbox" on the express. It was too late. The train had already rumbled past that tower, and was on its way to tragedy.

The burning wheel bearing locked in the journal, the seventh car was severed from the train, was jolted into the vertical, and was catapulted into a signal bridge framework. As it came to rest, the steel frame of the bridge tore the car to shreds. Those inside didn't stand a chance.

Wires on the signal bridge snapped. Sparks flew, high-voltage lines sprayed over the scene, and chaos broke out as seven cars which were trailing the afflicted coach were hurled off the tracks.

The uninjured servicemen scattered across the wreck site to maintain order and offer aid. Rapidly, emergency crews responded to the wreck, and even the most seasoned of them could not have expected what they found.

Four full blocks were strewn with debris. Hundreds of passengers lay moaning and crying, in agony over their injuries. Bodies of the dead were stacked and prepared for transport to a makeshift morgue in the basement of Frankford Hospital.

Stories of agony and escape were told and retold. There was the tale of Christina Nix, a New Yorker who was pried from the wreck after being trapped in the shredded steel for more than five hours. As she was lifted from the wreck, she repeatedly said, "Thank God I'm Irish!" Her luck ran out the next day when she was pronounced dead.

Morris Borden wasn't listed among the 80 who

died in the crash, but he was an indirect victim just the same. He had received word in his Brooklyn home that his wife and two children had been in a train accident in Philadelphia. All he could do when he arrived at the scene was identify their corpses.

All he could do when he returned home, alone and an emotionally-broken man, was turn on the gas jets of his kitchen range, close the kitchen windows, and breathe until he could breathe no more.

The carnage might have been avoided if, as the Interstate Commerce Commission noted in its report on recent rail accidents, "the urge to keep trains moving were not permitted to take precedence over safety."

Despite the importance of the Washington-Philadelphia-New York rail corridor, despite the reputation of a train such as the Congressional Limited, and despite recent technological advancements, communications on the route were primitive.

Something as simple, and as economical as a two-way radio setup may well have enabled that switcher engineer to contact the next signalman in time to alert the engineer of the Limited of the "hotbox."

***

June 15, 1945
Milton, Northumberland County

Private First Class Herb Swan was enjoying his first taste of freedom in more than two years.

The Buffalo, New York, soldier was headed home at last from Washington, where he had been transferred after his release from a prisoner-of-war camp in Germany.

PFC Swan had been captured by the Nazis in February, 1943, in North Africa. His family was to meet him at the Buffalo station that night, and the reunion would be charged with joy.

His parents waited, and waited. Word finally reached them that the Dominion Express, on which their soldier-son was traveling, had been involved in an accident near Milton, Pennsylvania. More information would be forthcoming.

They waited longer. A relief train arrived in Buffalo. Their boy was not on it.

Their wait, and their joy, ended, when they received a call at their home that their son was one of 19 who died in that train wreck.

It was another wreck caused by a "hotbox."

The express, Pennsylvania Railroad train No 575, which that day in June was pulling 14 cars from the nation's capital to Buffalo, was rolling along at top speed when, without warning, its engine slammed into a derailed car in the middle of a southbound freight on the opposite tracks.

The car had been knocked off the tracks after a journal had broken. The conductor of the freight train had stopped to assess the damage and post a warning flag when the express zoomed by.

With a thunderous roar, the engine plowed into the afflicted car, and took 20 more freight cars and seven of its own coaches into a massive pileup.

Private First Class Lester Calvert, who survived the wreck, said the resulting crash was, "louder than anything I heard on European battlefronts."

It was the last sound Private Swan, and 18 fellow people, ever heard.

***

January 18, 1946
Myerstown, Lebanon County
May 28, 1946
Middletown, Dauphin County

The war was over, but the fickle finger of the Grim Reaper was yet to select more casualties.

They would not fall on battlefields in a distant land, but on railroad lines right around the corner from their homes.

On January 18, 1946, the Navy Department

released the names of more than 100 sailors whose casualty status was changed from "missing in action" to "dead." Thousands more soldiers and sailors were being mustered out of the service and were heading home.

A train carrying soldiers from the 29th Infantry Division was approaching Lebanon, on its way from Camp Kilmer to Camp Shelby, Mississippi, when it collided with a Reading freight train. More than 20 passengers, including 16 soldiers, were injured. The fireman of the troop train and one soldier died.

Four months later, a Pennsylvania Railroad troop train, carrying 208 Marines bound for discharge at Bainbridge, Maryland, derailed on a spur east of Harrisburg.

More than 30 of the Pacific War veterans sustained injuries, and two of them were killed. The engineer, Clarence Merget, of Philadelphia, was scalded to death by steam in the cab of the engine.

MURDER AT VALLEY FORGE
May 9, 1948
Valley Forge, Montgomery County

The Sunday night special train lumbered slowly along the Schuylkill, through Valley Forge Park, carrying 50 passengers from Allentown to Philadelphia.

Just before nine o'clock, as the train pulled out of the Valley Forge Station after leaving 40 passengers off, it headed for a stretch of the Reading line where four sets of tracks paralleled the river. At once, engineer Buck Demmy was startled when his locomotive lurched, twisted, and fell from the rails.

Demmy stayed at the throttle, and was unable to save himself. The camelback rolled on its side, killing Demmy instantly.

Fireman Howard Jackson suffered an even more grisly fate. Trapped in the tender as it leaped from the tracks in a split-second of time, his body was found under eight tons of coal.

As the baggage car and two coaches were pulled from the rails by the momentum of the falling engine and tender, passengers scrambled, screamed and scraped around the overturned cars. Fortunately, none was injured seriously. The speed of the train, estimated to be slower than 30 miles per hour, doubtlessly contributed to the good fortune of the people in the cars.

Conductor Harold Kooker ran from the scene, looking for an emergency telephone somewhere along the tracks. His call sent emergency response crews rushing to the scene.

Park police Sgt. Charles Dickens and park guard Roy Hildebrand found their way through the graveyard of the Washington Memorial Chapel, and then through thick underbrush to the scene of the wreck.

Soon, rescue workers arrived en masse. Powerful floodlights cast an eerie glow on the scene, and gawkers turned up by the hundreds.

Some of the more seriously injured were treated at the park guard barracks, others were treated at a Norristown hospital, and most continued their journey to Philadelphia on a local which stopped at the scene.

As wrecks go, except for the tragic deaths of the crewmen, the Valley Forge accident was not of historical proportions.

But from the start of the probe into the cause of the mishap, investigators felt something was awry.

Montgomery County Coroner Winslow Rushong disclosed that bolts had been cut from a tie plate. He asked the Pennsylvania State Police and county District Attorney E. Arnold Forrest to join in the inquiry.

The next day, Reading Railroad officials confirmed that the wreck was the act of sabotage. The rail had been torn up by a three-foot long wrench and a huge pull bar which had been stolen from a tool shed near the scene.

Specifically, the railroad issued this statement:

The spikes had been pulled from both sides for an entire rail length and the tie plate upon which the rail rests had been removed from the end of the rail.

The rail, however, had been left in place and the bond wires which connect the ends of the rails and through which current flows to control track signals had not been broken, thus permitting a proceed signal to be given to the engineer.

The cause seemed clear. The effect was tragic. The motive was elusive.

The technique employed by the culprit or culprits indicated clearly, as it had in the Bryn Athyn Wreck of 1921, that they knew if the signal wires had been cut, the wreck would probably not have happened.

Thus, investigators labeled the derailment "deliberate murder," and went about gathering evidence.

Track worker Harold White of Philadelphia came forth with a raincoat, rolled up and tied with a rope, which he had found stuffed into a hole in the ground near the scene of the wreck. It was theorized the coat could have been used to hide the stolen tools.

The track foreman said the rails had been routinely inspected the day before the fatal wreck, and were in fine condition. After he was summoned to the scene the night of the derailment, he discovered broken windows in the tool shed, and that tools had been taken.

Intensive questioning of all who worked along that section revealed that there had been some unrest in labor camps at Bridgeport and Perkiomen Junction. Two workers were fired three days before the wreck, and six other had quit in a dispute over the quality of food in the camp.

The Reading offered a $500 reward for information leading to the arrest and conviction of the perpetrators, and the investigation continued.

It was discovered that a train had traveled over the same rails at about 60 miles per hour only 60 minutes before the wreck. That pinpointed the time of the dirty work of the wrecker.

Still, the disposition of the stolen tools, and an exact motive remained a mystery.

The Interstate Commerce Commission was conducting its own investigation at the Reading Company YMCA in Reading, and because 70 spikes, 23 tie plates and several angle bars had been removed, it was reasoned the deed must have been done by more than one man, and those familiar with railroading. And yet, any true railroader would have known that far less tampering

183

would have also caused the derailment.

The investigation went into a stall for months. While the police, the D.A., the coroner, the railroad, the I.C.C. and the public all knew the when, the what, the where and the how, the who and why were unresolved.

By June, the railroad upped the reward ante to $5,000.

There were still no takers.

The authorities had a few suspects. Some had been questioned, and some were long gone from the area after their dismissals from the labor gangs.

One of those who had been on the list of those sought for questioning was James M. Johnson, a 30-year old native of Pocomoke City, Maryland, who had a history of personal problems with and violence toward railroads.

In 1940, he was convicted of derailing a train in Delaware, and had served seven years in jail. The far-reaching investigation in Montgomery County had reached that far and that far back into the files of anyone who may have reason to cause a wreck.

Johnson was minding his own business, but unfortunately for him, walking against traffic on a highway near Edgefield, South Carolina on November 11, 1948. Local police picked him up for the minor violation, and checked his finger prints.

They discovered he was wanted by police in Montgomery County as a suspect in the May derailment, based on his crime eight years prior.

Johnson was taken to Norristown, where, as they said in old movies, "he sang like a bird."

He uttered and signed a five-page confession, describing in great detail the scene, the technique he employed, and finally, his motive.

Simply put, Johnson was hoping for many deaths that night so he could loot the corpses' clothing for money and valuables.

He was shocked when almost every passenger

184

limped out of the wrecked cars, and showed few signs of serious injury. He ran from the scene.

Johnson was arrested for murder in the first degree, and convicted after a trial in March, 1949. The jury recommended death in the electric chair.

He was granted a retrial on a technicality, and a new jury on October 6, 1951 re-convicted him but recommended life in prison.

***

May 16, 1948
Delaware Water Gap, Monroe County

Death came to one of the most picturesque stretches of railroad in Pennsylvania early Sunday morning when the engine and baggage car of the mail train from Hoboken to Buffalo slipped from the rails and slid down a steep embankment into the Delaware River.

The Lackawanna Railroad train was rounding a graceful curve through the Delaware Water Gap shortly after midnight. There were no passengers on the Saturday-only run which was loaded chiefly with Sunday newspapers.

Its engineer and fireman both perished in the accident.

***

September 20, 1949
Pottsville, Schuylkill County

A ten-car Reading Railroad train, traveling to Shamokin from Philadelphia, approached a grade crossing between Port Carbon and Palo Alto as a Unity Oil Co. tank truck filled with 4,500 gallons of gasoline apparently attempted to beat the train.

It did not.

With an explosive force which swept across three

train cars, caused fires in automobiles and nearby buildings, and threw fireman Kenneth Beck from his train "like a human torch," the truck blew up.

All passengers on the train escaped injury, but Beck and two other men, including the truck driver, were killed instantly.

MAYHEM ON THE MAIN LINE
May 18, 1951
Villanova, Delaware County

It happened in the early morning sunshine, on one of the most storied and busiest railroad lines in the United States.

It left nine persons dead, more than 60 hurting, and an engineer under arrest.

The Red Arrow, the crack Pennsylvania Railroad electric train which crossed the east from Detroit to New York, was pulling ten cars as it rolled past commuter stations along the Main Line which stretches through the affluent western suburbs of Philadelphia.

It was the same Red Arrow flyer which, four years before, had derailed on a mountainous curve near Altoona, killing 24 passengers.

That morning on the Main Line, the express was inching away from a red signal at Villanova. Down the tracks, near Roberts Road between the Rosemont and Bryn Mawr stations, the Philadelphia Night Express, returning to the city from Pittsburgh, had been stopped by an automatic signal after a piece of equipment had fallen from beneath one of its 19 coaches, tripping an equipment detector bar and setting off the stop signal.

The flagman of the Night Express positioned himself to warn any oncoming trains of the hazard, and by all indications, the engineer of the Red Arrow was well aware of the situation. The block signal system had warned him of the presence of the Night Express.

187

Investigators were mystified at the outset at how the accident could have happened, all things considered.

But it happened, and the 238-ton electric engine of the Red Arrow slammed into the express with such force that the Poplar Vale and Cascade Chasm, two solid Pullmans, were virtually demolished by the impact. All of those who died were in the Poplar Vale, the last car of the Night Express. Most were still asleep when the collision took place.

The Pullmans joined the express at Harrisburg, after being left there by the Clevelander.

Samuel Miller was a waiter in the dining car of the Red Arrow when the crash took place. "Everything seemed to go up in the air. I looked out of the pantry and saw that tables, food and the 14 persons in the diner were in a shambles," he stated.

The roar of the collision echoed through the neighborhood. Busy Lancaster Avenue was clogged quickly as motorists stopped to see whatever they could see. The wreck scene became so packed with spectators that 60 officers from Lower Merion Township were called in as other towns sent policemen, the State Police dispatched troopers, and Military Police from the Schuylkill Barracks were deployed.

The Salvation Army, Red Cross, and surrounding churches and businesses provided transportation, first-aid units, emergency equipment and provisions for the rescue workers. Dozens of students from Villanova and other schools near the site donated blood in an emergency appeal from the Red Cross and Bryn Mawr Hospital.

At first, both the engineer and fireman of the Red Arrow were reported to have been killed in the crash. Bill Ferris, who lived in a nearby apartment complex, knew otherwise. The 25-year old ran to the scene and helped pull Frank Yentzer, the 62-year old engineer, and Clarence Ward, the 44-year old fireman, from the wreck.

The sound of the crash caught Bob O'Connor in mid-shave in his Bryn Mawr home that morning. The former Philadelphia Eagles football player slipped on a coat and ran to the scene to help lead the injured from the rubble.

After erroneously being reported as dead, Yentzer, a 25-year P.R.R. veteran from Harrisburg, was taken to Bryn Mawr Hospital and given a thorough examination. It was so thorough that it revealed that he had virtually no vision in his right eye. The examining physician did say the impairment could have been caused by injuries sustained in the accident.

Still, the revelation was cause for concern. Pennsylvania Railroad officials quickly pointed out that all its engineers' eyes are examined every three to six months, and even if Yentzer's condition predated the crash, there is a whistle in the cab which augments the visual stop or slow-down signals.

Yentzer did say he followed all signals as he brought his train around a curve and into the path of the Night Express. His signal switched to warn him to proceed slower than 45 miles per hour, and he reasoned it was given because the Red Arrow would be diverting to another track at Bryn Mawr.

Instead, as the train rolled into Rosemont, Clarence Ward saw the stop signal, and Yentzer gave the Red Arrow all the braking power he could.

Yentzer maintained that there was a problem with the signal devices in his cab. Later tests by the railroad disputed that, and officials claimed both the cab and wayside signal systems were working fine.

Nearly a month after the accident, the Interstate Commerce Commission handed down a ruling at the conclusion of its investigation.

The Pennsylvania Railroad was instructed to install a more modern, automatic speed-control system on that section of its line. The system would automatically bring the speeds of all trains to 20 miles per hour when another train is in the same block.

The railroad agreed to comply with that

recommendation.

Still, the exact cause of the Main Line wreck was unclear until later in the summer of 1951.

The inquiry concluded that Yentzer had been responsible for the wreck, and on June 27, he was charged with involuntary manslaughter.

While Yentzer took the fall for the crash, another unanswered question may have been answered, with a most unlikely and bizarre culprit at its root.

What, in the first place, caused the Night Express to trip the signal bar on the tracks? What piece of equipment was dangling from its undercarriage?

The engineer of the Night Express had testified that he had personally inspected the underside of his train after the wreck, to see what might have dragged along the ground, setting off the stop signal.

All he found was the carcass of a crow. The wreck on the Main Line that spring, a wreck which killed nine people, may have been touched off by a dead crow!

***

June 4, 1951
Chalfont, Bucks County

It was truly a joyous weekend for the Buda family of Brooklyn, New York.

Alfred and Augustine Buda had celebrated their 25th wedding anniversary on Friday, and their daughter had graduated that morning from Harcourt Junior College in Swarthmore.

What's more, it was Patricia's 19th birthday that Saturday!

The Brooklyn doctor, his wife, two daughters, a niece and a nephew were returning home along Route 202 after the graduation ceremonies when a Reading Railroad train plowed into their car at a grade crossing and put an abrupt end to their short-lived joy.

Dr. and Mrs. Buda were killed, and their passengers, including Patricia, were injured.

A RUNAWAY RAMPAGE
May 30, 1953
Lancaster

This one will test the imagination of anyone who has ever read any details of any train wreck at any time.

A 13-car freight train was shuttling slowly on tracks which ran in the center of Water Street, in the heart of downtown Lancaster.

Never more than a few blocks from Penn Square, in the very heart of the city, the Pennsylvania Railroad train was dropping off various cargoes at shops and factories in town.

Directly in back of the engine was the caboose, and the freight cars were strung behind the caboose. The entire crew was assembled in the cab and the caboose, and had no idea what had happened at the far end of their train that afternoon.

Somehow, presumably at a faulty switch, the last car of the train was derailed. It remained coupled to the rest of the train, but slid off the tracks and onto the street.

For a full three blocks, the car was towed by an unknowing crew up front, and for a full three blocks, the wavering car wreaked havoc on everything in its path.

The first victims were parked cars. As the car skidded along the macadam, it crushed car after car, until 17 vehicles were reduced to ruin. One of them was brand new, with about 90 miles on its odometer. It was totaled.

Residents in homes along Water Street watched in stunned shock as the wobbling, wayward car took down fire escapes, porches, parking meters and anything else unfortunate enough to be in its way.

Someone called the Lancaster Police, and two patrol cars were dispatched to the neighborhood to stop the train. By the time the officers arrived, they discovered something most bizarre.

The engineer had finally brought his train to a halt at Water and Conestoga Streets, but not because of the renegade car.

For some strange reason, a 38-year old man had decided to take a mid-day nap between the rails of the Water Street tracks. Unable to roust the man, the engineer stopped the train.

When the officers caught up with the engineer, they told him of the escapades of the car. They walked to the end of the train to discover that the car had somehow righted itself and returned to the rails.

The only proof of its rampage was a three-block long swath of destruction.

* * *

Armistice Day, November 11, 1953
Philadelphia

Passenger volume that day was light because of the holiday. And that fact may have played a role in keeping casualties to a minimum when a Pennsylvania Railroad commuter train demolished a switch and slammed into a cement wall on the approach to the Thirtieth Street Station.

The eight-car train was on its way to the Suburban Station, a short and slow run. But, as the electric engine ventured from track 2 to track 1, the switch was split and the first coach reared up against the wall and came down on a steel railing between the two sets of tracks. The girder sliced the coach in two, and the second car followed the first into the wall.

Miraculously, none of the 30 passengers in the two cars was seriously injured.

THE WRECK OF THE BASEBALL SPECIAL
July 28, 1962
Steelton, Dauphin County

It was to be a grand night at the ball park for hundreds of fans of either the Philadelphia Phillies or Pittsburgh Pirates. A "Baseball Special" train had pulled out of Harrisburg on the Pennsylvania line shortly after five o'clock that Saturday night, with 120 people crowded into three of its nine cars. The other cars would be filled with more people at stops along the way to Philadelphia.

The train was only minutes out of the capital when engineer J.F. Shue opened her up to about 70 miles per hour. The limit was 75 m.p.h. on that straightaway to the rear of the Bethlehem Steel plant in Steelton.

All was well for precious few moments until, as a witness said, "I saw the engine and five cars go by, but the sixth caught a pole."

He was David Wilbert, a foreman at the steel plant who happened to be looking out a window when the excursion train zoomed by.

"It kept on going and hit a second and third pole before it fishtailed and went down the embankment."

Three of the cars wound up down the steep, 40-foot hill and into the Susquehanna River. Two cars were derailed, but remained upright.

At the bottom of the embankment, and in the river, dozens of people were trapped in the overturned cars, and in four feet of water.

193

As the cars careened off the tracks, they took down high-voltage lines, and those wires sparked brush fires which had to be beaten back before rescuers could reach the wreckage from the track level.

Meanwhile, help on land, river and in the air was summoned. Helicopters from Olmsted Air Force base, just down the road, helped pull survivors from the river, while skin divers and passing boaters provided their special services on the water.

The smoke from the wreck spiraled high in the sky, and could be seen for many miles around.

When a barge on the river pulled the last body out well after midnight, the final count was 19 dead, and about 116 injured. It was the worst train wreck in the country since a 1958 crash in Bayonne, N.J.

The investigation which followed the wreck determined that a railroad work crew which was working on the tracks did not install enough rail anchors to keep the rails in alignment. The crew of the excursion had noticed the misalignment, and was trying to slow the train down just as it derailed.

The following year, family members of eight of the 19 who died on the express filed claims of almost $1.5 million against the Pennsylvania Railroad.

Legal and technical details aside, a poignant sight was noticed by rescuers as they searched for the dead and eased the wounds of the injured.

Slipping through the windows of the coaches, which rested on their side in the river, were pennants. Dozens of red pennants, emblazoned "Phillies," floated silently down the river.

For many of those on the Baseball Express that night, it was to be their very first trip to a major league baseball game.

Some never made it.

***

August 14, 1962
Coatesville, Chester County

The headline was a bit frightening. "Train With Atom Cargo Hit By Another, Killing 2 Men."

But, when one read beyond The New York Times' banner, it was discovered that the Pennsylvania Railroad freighter was transporting a low-level atomic cargo and definitely not weapons material.

The Atomic Energy Commission was still tight-lipped about the substance, while it was hinted it was likely nuclear submarine fuel.

The train was stopped at a maintenance site along the way when another freight slammed into it. Two crewmen on the second train were killed.

There was no danger of a radiation release.

***

January 21, 1963
Philadelphia

What a start of a new year! President John F. Kennedy was calling for a tax cut to help stimulate a sagging economy; Walt Disney and Henry Ford were putting the final touches on plans for the 1964 World's Fair; Teamsters boss Jimmy Hoffa braved five-degree temperatures in Philadelphia to help organize area truckers; and the Philadelphia Transportation Company (PTC) was seeking immediate permission from regulating authorities for a fare hike which would make the cost of riding a Philly bus or trolley a whopping 25 cents!

The PTC needed the infusion of cash because members of the Transport Workers Union were requesting a pay raise, to an unheard-of $2.86 per hour!

And while the PTC and TWU lawyers and business agents battled things out at the negotiating table, a citywide transit strike had created gridlock on city streets and chaos on Reading Railroad commuter trains.

The problems faced by commuters was complicated further at eight o'clock on a Monday morning when two Reading commuter trains, each at standing-room-only capacity, collided near the Spring Garden Station on north Broad Street.

Of the 1,500 passengers on the four cars of the Jenkintown shuttle and six cars of the Chestnut Hill local, 279 were shaken up enough to require medical attention. There were no fatalities.

There were lots of emergency vehicles on the scene in a flash. More than 60 police cars showed up, and the fire department sent six rescue squads, a ladder company and a pumper.

In a strange sense, the accident couldn't have happened at a better time for the staff at St. Luke's and Children's Hospital. Just months ago, the hospital, which is only a block from the Reading's main line, staged a mock railroad disaster drill as part of its regular training program.

Cuts, serious bruises and broken bones kept 18 victims in hospitals, while more than 260 others were treated and released.

Meanwhile, the transit situation raged on in the streets and the conference rooms of the city.

The final verdict of a board of inquiry after the crash indicated that the electric brakes of the Jenkintown shuttle failed, and the emergency brakes were not strong enough to stop the overloaded train on the slight downgrade.

FROM COALS TO TOXINS
Train Wrecks in the Modern Era

There was a time when the major fears in train wrecks were toppled stoves as fire hazards and spilled coals as marginal environmental hazards.

There was a time when scandals broke out when it was discovered the engineer or conductor of a wrecked train was found with liquor on his breath.

There was a time when dilapidated equipment and waysides were major contributors to train wrecks.

My, how things have changed. My, how things have stayed the same.

Sadly, the classic images of powerful railroad companies, steam engines, steel rails and iron men faded as the third quarter of the twentieth century opened.

Familiar freight train liveries and logos were painted over by Conrail blue and much of the passenger service between cities was transferred to Amtrak, or abandoned entirely.

If nothing else, the safety record on the rails was greatly improved, and the stories of wholesale loss of life began to fade from the headlines.

But, new challenges and new threats rode the rails of Eastern Pennsylvania.

Government intervention, regulation, deregulation and re-regulation cast long shadows on rail traffic. And, sociological problems became factors in the personnel, equipment and cargoes of railroads.

Through the 1970s, worries mounted over the

197

dangers posed by the railroads' transporting of toxic chemicals. Anxieties about pollution and poisoning created many perils, both real and imagined.

February 17, 1976; Trainer, Delaware County: Five blocks of the town were evacuated after a Penn Central tank car began to leak the flammable, toxic, carbon disulfide. The 350 residents were later allowed to return home after the liquid was transferred to another car.

November 28, 1977; West Philadelphia: After ten cars of a 91-car Conrail freight derailed, fire officials ordered the evacuation of more than 200 residents. Firemen feared the leakage of poisonous gases from two tank cars which had overturned, but there was no leak, and residents went back to their homes within three hours.

January 14, 1978; Pond Eddy, Pike County: A tank car filled with acetaldehyde, split apart and drained the chemical into the Delaware River. The spill resulted in the evacuation of a four square mile area on both the New York and Pennsylvania sides of the river. Residents said the chemical created a "fruity" smell when it leaked. The sweet odor was deceiving, however. The liquid is highly explosive, and can cause severe irritation to humans if they come into contact with it.

November 11, 1978; Sharon Hill, Delaware County: More than 1,000 people were routed from their homes when a derailment resulted in the spill of sulphuric acid. They returned home after an overnight cleanup operation.

August 19, 1979; Philadelphia: Acetone spilled on a street in the Kensington section when a Conrail tanker derailed and ruptured. Firefighters neutralized the substance, and all was well.

January 15, 1980; Philadelphia: Fire crews rushed to the scene of a derailment in north Philadelphia, after toxic chemical fumes spewed from an overturned tank car. About 200 nearby residents were evacuated.

198

April 12, 1980; Quarryville, Lancaster County:
Three dozen cars on a Conrail freight derailed, and
authorities feared the spill of a toxic substance. Two cars
did break apart, but they leaked only a harmless
refrigeration gas.

The scares, the fears, and the realities of railroads
in the 1970s kept government, industry, the railroads and
the public on edge, and instilled in all their consciences the
need to guard against possible catastrophes which could
far eclipse any train wrecks of the nineteenth and early
twentieth centuries.

What could have been a monumental disaster was
averted on October 17, 1979 on the commuter rail tracks
between the Angora and 49th Street stations in
Philadelphia.

As Lester Shank was bringing his four-car train in
from Delaware County he noticed a caution signal ahead
and applied the brakes. Suddenly, a crewman yelled to
him that there was a stop signal displayed ahead of the
caution light. Shank threw the door of the car open and
shouted to the passengers, "Brace yourselves!" He was
hitting the brakes at full force, but still knew it was too
late.

The Southeastern Pennsylvania Transportation
Authority (SEPTA) 7:50 from Elwyn, slammed into the
two-car 7:07 from West Chester, which had stopped on
the tracks while two trains from Media were shifting cars.

George Faust, conductor of the 7:07, which was
waiting for the first to shuffle its cars, was seriously
injured when his train was sandwiched by the collision.
He died of those injuries the following week.

A total of 442 passengers were injured in the 17-
car chain reaction crash, and 26 were admitted to
hospitals. The accident, which took place in the middle of
the Tuesday morning rush hour, drew hundreds of
emergency workers, and thousands of spectators.

"There was no screaming," said Robert Burke, a
passenger on the commuter. "There was a kind of

stunned silence. A lot of people were bleeding from the mouth."

About half of those who were shaken up were taken to a nearby elementary school which became a makeshift field hospital.

"A lot of seats came off their hinges, ripped off or buckled," noted J.A. Rowdon, another passenger, who said the impact sounded like "two big shudders."

But Mary Brenenborg, who was in the third train, summed up the incident with some whimsy. "I'll tell you one thing," she said, "that wreck beat the hell out of a cup of coffee for waking me up!"

As the busy commuter line was being cleaned up, the injured were nursing their wounds, and the conductor was being buried, railroad accident investigators swung into action.

They re-created the mishap, and theorized that several factors, from human error to equipment failure, may have contributed to the crash.

Ironically, as the probe for the cause of that accident continued, yet another incident occurred on the same SEPTA line.

A circuit-breaker fire during the afternoon rush hour two days after the big crash totally shut down all electric train service in center-city Philadelphia. An electric substation was ravaged by a $1 million fire.

The cause for the fire was a squirrel which had ventured into the wiring and short-circuited the system. "Its hair was totally burned off," said a SEPTA spokesperson, "and there we had it, dead proof."

The public's confidence in and patience with the passenger rail network, or what was left of it, had been further strained. Most riders of the Media local line, on which the three-train crash had occurred, had been calling their train "The Clunker" for months, and for obvious reasons.

There was an uneasy dichotomy developing in southeastern Pennsylvania. The commuter lines were the convenient, and usually reliable lifelines for hundreds of thousands of people going to and from work. Yet, those lines were becoming notoriously unsafe.

November 14, 1979; Upper Darby, Delaware County: A fire, thought to be electrical in origin, broke out on a SEPTA train, filling a one-car commuter train and sickening and singeing more than 50 passengers.

November 30, 1979; Royersford, Montgomery County: Two Conrail crewmen died when a coal train collided with a 115-car freight train which had stopped awaiting a signal at the entrance to a tunnel. SEPTA commuter service was disrupted because of the wreckage.

July 17, 1980; North Wales, Montgomery County: Mechanical problems caused one commuter train to stop on the tracks while a second slammed into it. More than 70 passengers were injured and four cars were derailed.

It was a period of transition for the vast network of commuter lines in and around Philadelphia.

The Northeast Railway Transit Act of 1981 shifted operation of the lines from Conrail to SEPTA on January 1, 1983. Conrail, literally the CONsolidation of eight northeastern RAILroads which had gone bankrupt, thus could concentrate on freight service.

What SEPTA inherited, however, were shabby, sad relics of a bygone era. It was expected to run a modern and safe commuter system with pitifully outdated equipment and a crumbling infrastructure on 255 miles of heavily-used passenger routes.

Old Reading and Pennsylvania railroad roadbeds, bridges and rolling stock, plus brand-new problems coming out of union halls and governmental chambers created myriad headaches for the new transit authority.

After SEPTA inspectors looked closely at what it had received from Conrail, they were appalled. A 73-year old bridge in Philadelphia that supported six former Reading Company lines was so rusty that a person's thumb could punch a hole in parts of it. Above it were the six railroad lines. Beneath it was a building used as a community center. It was a disaster waiting to happen.

All 434 bridges in outlying towns and townships needed repairs, and 24 were termed unsafe. In 1980 alone, 350 passenger cars were put into service despite charges that they should not have been because they were in dire disrepair. That same year, more than 1,700 notices of defective trackage were issued to Conrail by the Federal Railroad Administration.

At the root of it, the fledgling transit authority and Conrail both charged and counter-charged, was inadequate funding.

Big money was freed up for what Philadelphia politicians called the savior of the system, a $330 million commuter rail tunnel which would link the 30th Street Station and Reading Terminal, and thereby join the former Reading and Pennsylvania rail lines in a united commuter rail system.

While the tunnel was a political football for years, and the object of countless controversies during its construction, it really did serve a valuable function.

In fact, when it was opened to much fanfare on November 12, 1984, Mayor W. Wilson Goode said it was the crowning glory of "the most improved, most advanced transportation in the whole country."

Nine days after he uttered those hopeful words, 140 passengers were slightly injured when two SEPTA trains collided at the Narberth Station.

This time, it wasn't a squirrel, or a signal, or a brake which was blamed. The rails were wet, and slippery. Simple as that.

Still, the traditional causes of train wrecks continued to vex those who were to ride the rails into the twenty-first century.

February 20, 1975; Leacock Township, Lancaster County: A one-car Amtrak commuter with six passengers en route from Harrisburg to Philadelphia plowed into a truck at an unguarded rail crossing east of Lancaster. The passengers, and the truck driver, sustained injuries.

December 26, 1976; Downingtown, Chester County: Nearly two dozen passengers were shaken up as four of the five cars of the Broadway Limited derailed after leaving Philadelphia.

Amtrak estimated 200 people were on board the train when it ran off the track. Most injuries were minor.

The train was going more than 70 miles per hour at the time, and investigators said deteriorated crossties caused the rails to move, causing the derailment.

Notice the changes in the preceding stories and paragraphs: A train going more than 70 miles per hour; a one-car train carrying six passengers; deteriorating ties; Conrail; Amtrak; bankruptcy; unions; funding.

Inter-city bus and commuter air service had taken over the bulk of passenger service by the 1980s, and trucks were carrying much of what railroads once did. Although Amtrak still served passengers on the former Pennsylvania Railroad and Conrail handled what was left of the freight business, railroads had become quaint anachronisms to most people.

Old stations were demolished or left to rot and fall. A fortunate few were preserved as restaurants and gift shops. Cabooses, eventually phased out altogether, were used as motel units and in town parks. One even turned up in front of a McDonald's in Womelsdorf, Berks County.

Hundreds of them were stored, like mothballed ships after a war, in rail yards in Reading.

And then, something wonderful happened. The memories of the people and the relics of the road were dusted off, spruced up, and put on display for all to revel in and ride upon.

Those who knew, and those who cared, toiled to keep the spirit of railroading alive. Rail excursions, tourist short lines, clubs, historical societies, and museums provided fuel to fire up the imaginations and curiosities of people who may never have even seen a real steam locomotive without their tireless efforts.

In a certain sense, the Golden Age of Railroading has come back. It may be only a reflection of that gilded time, but it shines on new faces in familiar places throughout Eastern Pennsylvania, truly the heartland of American railroading history.

ABOUT THE AUTHORS

This is the ninth collaboration of Charles J. Adams III and David J. Seibold. Previous subjects of their work range from ghost stories and legends to shipwrecks and sea stories.

Adams is also the author of three books on ghosts in his native Berks County.

Adams is the morning personality at WEEU radio in Reading, and is the Reading Eagle newspaper's chief travel correspondent.

He is past president of the Reading Public Library and also sits on the executive council and editorial board of the Historical Society of Berks County. He is a member of the board of directors of the Penn State Alumni Society of the Berks Campus, the Boyertown Museum of Historic Vehicles, the Exeter Township Historical Commission and several other community groups in Berks County. He is also listed in Who's Who in American Entertainment.

Adams has also composed and performed several railroad folk songs which are available on cassette tapes.

Seibold is a native of Willow Grove, and is an avid scuba diver and fisherman. He divides his time between homes in Reading and Barnegat Light, N.J.

A graduate of Penn State, Seibold is a member of the Barnegat Light Scuba and Rescue Team and operates his own charter boat. he is a former commodore of the Rajah Temple Yacht Club and is a decorated Vietnam Campaign veteran.

Seibold is employed as a senior account executive at WEEU radio, and is active in many civic and social organizations. He is a member of the Reading Company Technical and Historical Society.

Rev. Philip K. Smith (the "Rail Riding Pastor") grew up in Berne, near the Main Line of the Reading Company. He graduated Magna cum Laude from Muhlenberg College, where he had been elected to Phi Beta Kappa. In 1979, he received his Master of Divinity degree from Union Theological Seminary in New York City.

He is a member of the Train Collectors Association and the Hawk Mountain Chapter of the National Railway Historical Society. He has written and edited several books about toy trains for the Greenberg Publishing Company. His articles have been published in the Train Collectors Association Quarterly and O Gauge Railroading, a bimonthly magazine. He contributed to *Steam Locomotives of the Reading and P & R Railroads,* a thorough history of locomotives by class including 30 foldout plates, by Edward H. Wiswesser, P.E.

Co-authors David J. Seibold (left) and Charles J. Adams III.

GREAT TRAIN WRECKS OF EASTERN PENNSYLVANIA PHOTO GALLERY

THE END OF "TELESCOPE" ACCIDENTS?

A GREAT INVENTION.

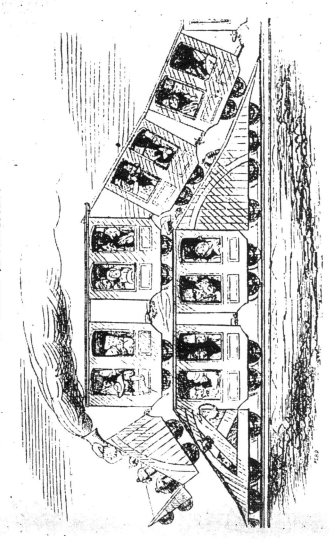

A BIZARRE CONTRAPTION WHICH WOULD FRAME PASSENGER CARS WITH "UP" AND "DOWN" RAMPS CAME FROM THE MIND OF AN EDITORIAL CARTOONIST IN ABOUT 1850. THE NOT-TOO-SUBTLE COMMENTARY ENCOURAGED THE DIRECTORS OF THE ERIE AND HUDSON RIVER RAILROAD TO ADOPT THE "ANTI-COLLISION RAILROAD CARRIAGE."

Described as one of the most devastating "hotbox" accidents in American railroading history, the Labor Day, 1943, wreck of the crack "Congressional Limited" killed 80 and injured scores more in the Frankford section of Philadelphia. (Photo courtesy of the Historical Society of Pennsylvania)

A Lehigh Valley express, carrying some $250,000 in gold, was wrecked when it struck an abandoned automobile on tracks near Pittston on January 4, 1942. One person was killed and 13 were injured. (Top) The seven derailed cars are seen in an aerial view; (bottom) a wrecking crew uses a crane to lift the stricken locomotive from the bottom of an embankment. (Photo courtesy of the Historical Society of Pennsylvania)

Loaded with many home-bound World War II veterans, the Pennsylvania Railroad "Dominion Express" struck a derailed ore car and wrecked near Milton on June 15, 1945. Nineteen were killed and 30 were injured in the collision. (Photo courtesy of the Historical Society of Pennsylvania)

More than 200 U.S. Marines, headed for their discharges after action in the Pacific Theatre, were aboard this troop train when it left a spur 15 miles east of Harrisburg in 1946. The train's engineer and two Marines were killed in the wreck. (Photo courtesy of the Historical Society of Pennsylvania)

Survivors of a May 28, 1946 wreck of a troop train near Harrisburg climb from a car after the derailment. The train's engineer and two marines died in the crash. (Photo courtesy of the Historical Society of Pennsylvania)

Weeds grow high around the old Exeter Station of the Reading Railroad. In 1899, the station, now in a village named Lorane, was the site of a wreck which killed 29 passengers aboard an excursion train. (Photo by Charles J. Adams III)

THE DREADFUL ACCIDENT ON THE NORTH PENNSYLVANIA RAIL-ROAD.

About 14 miles above Philadelphia, on Thursday, July 17, 1856, at about 6 A.M., which resulted in the death of over SIXTY, and terribly wounding about ONE HUNDRED persons, excursionists of St. Michael's R. C. Church, Kensington. The Collision took place at Camp Hill Station, destroying both locomotives and burning up several cars, on which a number of people were consumed.

A wild depiction of the July 17, 1856 wreck near the Camp Hill Station (now Fellwick), Montgomery County. A special north-bound excursion train carrying hundreds of young people on a church outing collided with a down train, killing 59 and injuring 86. (Courtesy of the Historical Society of Montgomery County)

Rescuers tend to the injured and carry away the dead in the July, 1856, wreck of an excursion train near Camp Hill Station, Montgomery County. (Courtesy of the Historical Society of Mongtomery County)

The horrifying result of a "telescope" railroad accident is personified in this photograph of the wreckage at Mud Run, Carbon County, on October 10, 1888. More than 60 passengers were killed in the wreck on the Lehigh Valley line. (Courtesy of the Library of Congress)

(Top) A car of the Mt. Penn Gravity Railroad pauses at the former Tower Hotel atop Mt. Penn, Reading, before being set free to roll along the downhill tracks back to the city. A car similar to it wrecked on a hairpin turn of the road (bottom) in August, 1890, killing five and injuring 20.

An artist depicts the wreck of an express to Pottsville along the Schuylkill River near Shoemakersville, Berks County, in September, 1890. Twenty-two were killed in the collision. (Courtesy of the Historical Society of Berks County)

Wreckage is strewn on the embankment and in the Schuylkill River as rescue teams approach the tragic September, 1890, wreck which killed 22 people north of Shomakersville, Berks County. (Courtesy of the Historical Society of Berks County)

Spectators gather on a hillside above the September, 1890, wreck near Shoemakersville, as rescue workers probe the Schuylkill River for survivors and the remains of the 22 who died in the wreck. (Courtesy of the Historical Society of Berks County)

As dawn broke on the scene of the Shoemakersville Wreck, the devastation was incredible. (Courtesy of the Historical Society of Berks County)

As engineer Charles Billig brought his freight train out of the Flat Rock Tunnel on October 24, 1892, he looked up to see the Shamokin Express on a collision course with his train. Seven people were killed. The tunnel is still used, and visible from the Schuylkill Expressway opposite Manayunk. (Photo by Charles J. Adams III)

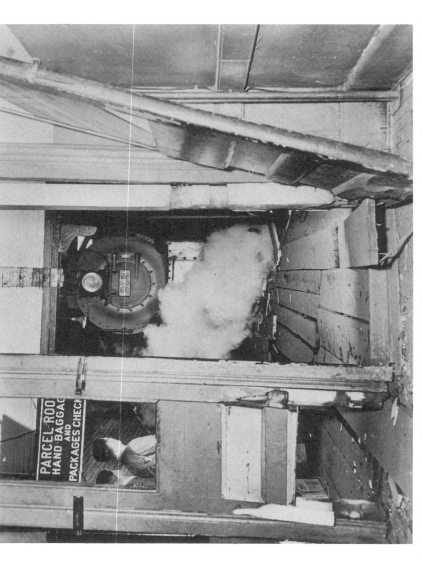

This incident on April 10, 1949 in Pottsville gives new meaning to the phrase, "a train pulling into the station." (Courtesy of the Schuylkill County Historical Society)

BIBLIOGRAPHY
BOOKS

The Guinness Railway Book, by John Marshall. Guinness Publishing Ltd., London, 1989

From Cab to Caboose, by Joseph A. Noble, University of Oklahoma Press, 1964

Journey Into Fear, Edited by Richard Peyton, Wings Books, New York, 1990

Scalded to Death by the Steam, by Katie Letcher Lyle, Algonquin Books of Chapel Hill, 1991

Disaster!, Edited by Ben Kartman & Leonard Brown, Pellegrini and Cudahy, 1948

The American Heritage History of Railroads in America,, by Oliver Jensen, American Heritage Publishing Co., 1975

Encyclopedia of North American Railroading, by Freeman H. Hubbard, McGraw-Hill, Inc., 1981

Long Steel Rail: The Railroad in American Folksong, by Norm Cohen, University of Illinois Press, 1981

Development of the Locomotive Engine, by Angus Sinclair, Angus Sinclair Publishing Co., 1907

The Montgomery County Story, by E. Gordon Alderfer

Centennial History of the Pennsylvania Railroad Company, 1846-1946, by George H. Burgess and Miles C. Kennedy. Pennsylvania Railroad Company, 1949.

NEWSPAPERS AND MAGAZINES

The New York Times, Reading Eagle, Reading Herald, Allentown Call-Chronicle, Philadelphia Inquirer, Philadelphia Bulletin, Bethlehem Globe, Norristown Weekly Herald, Philadelphia Public Ledger, The Scranton Republican, Munsey's Magazine, Railroad Magazine, Pottstown Mercury, Utica Globe, Pennsylvania History, American Railway, Harper's Weekly.

FACILITIES

Reading Public Library, Albright College Library, Allentown Public Library, Bethlehem Area Public Library, Kutztown University Library, Scranton University Library, Lehigh University Library, East Stroudsburg University Library, Library of Congress, Free Library of Philadelphia, Historical Society of Montgomery County, Historical Society of Berks County, Historical Society of Pennsylvania, Schuylkill County Historical Society, Reading Company Historical and Technical Society, Blue Mountain and Reading Railroad, Library Company of Philadelphia, Pennsylvania Railroad Museum, Strasburg Rail Road, Wanamaker, Kempton & Southern Railroad, Steamtown USA.

SPECIAL THANKS TO...

Jim Holton, author of the definitive history of the Reading Railroad; Bev Smith, Barbara Gill, in the library of the Historical Society of Berks County; Eileen O'Connor, Louise Jones and others at the Historical Society of Pennsylvania; Diane Fisher, John Joy at the Schuylkill County Historical Society, Debbie Schanzenbach, Phil Macaronis, Kirby Powell, Margie Bender, Ranger Bob Rice, Hickory Run State Park; Julie Ruskik, Jonathan L. Shalter III, Judith A.H. Meier, and especially our loved ones and families who remained patient during the making of this book.